The Power of Partnering:
A Blueprint for Collaborative Leadership

Building Cultures of Trust and Innovation

Zen Benefiel, MA, MBA

Publisher: Be The Dream Publishing

© 2024

ISBN: 9798340802361

Introduction: The Power of Partnering

In today's fast-paced, ever-evolving world, the way we work together is more critical than ever. Whether it's building a high-stakes construction project, navigating corporate dynamics, or collaborating across global teams, one truth remains clear: the success of any endeavor relies on the strength of its partnerships. Yet, in many workplaces, collaboration is often reduced to task-based coordination, leaving behind the deeper, more powerful connection that can transform teams from mere groups of people into aligned, purpose-driven units. This is where partnering becomes essential.

Partnering is not just a buzzword; it's a practice—a mindset that builds trust, encourages transparency, and creates a shared responsibility for success. It's about recognizing that no individual holds all the answers, but when we work together with open hearts and minds, we can accomplish far more than we ever could alone. Partnering invites us to break down silos, embrace collective accountability, and ensure that each person feels valued and heard. It's a holistic approach to teamwork, one that harmonizes the needs of the individual with the goals of the collective.

I've had the privilege of seeing firsthand how powerful partnering can be. From my work in aerospace, where precision and teamwork were critical, to managing large-scale events with thousands of moving parts, I learned that the most successful projects were those where communication was clear, expectations were aligned, and teams operated from a place of mutual respect. Later, through Team Partnering LLC, I helped bring partnering to the construction industry, where complex, high-pressure projects benefitted immensely from this collaborative approach.

But partnering doesn't stop at the organizational level. It's also a deeply personal practice. As I developed my holistic coaching programs and explored the spiritual dimensions of teamwork, I realized that true collaboration is about more than just getting the job done—it's about personal growth, self-awareness, and the willingness to see ourselves as part of something bigger.

Partnering becomes not just a tool for success, but a path toward harmony within ourselves and with those around us.

This book is about bringing those insights into the spotlight and showing how partnering can transform not only your projects but also your work environment and relationships. It's about fostering a culture where collaboration thrives, conflicts are resolved constructively, and everyone is invested in a shared vision. In the following chapters, we'll explore the principles of partnering from both a practical and holistic perspective, drawing from real-world examples and personal growth strategies to create a comprehensive guide for building better teams, achieving greater success, and creating lasting harmony in your work and life.

Whether you're a leader, a project manager, or a team member looking to enhance your role, the principles outlined in this book will offer you a fresh, powerful approach to collaboration. We'll cover everything from conflict resolution and communication to spiritual alignment and personal empowerment. As you read through these pages, you'll discover that partnering isn't just a technique—it's a philosophy for living and working in a way that is more connected, more purposeful, and ultimately, more fulfilling.

Welcome to the power of partnering. Let's explore how working together, in true harmony, can lead us to greater success and deeper satisfaction in every aspect of life.

Contents

Chapter 1: The Foundations of Partnering 1

Chapter 2: Solutions – A New Approach 7

Chapter 3: Navigating Holistic Growth 13

Chapter 4: A Tool for Conflict Resolution 19

Chapter 5: The Role of Servant Leadership 27

Chapter 6: Breaking Down Silos – Building Trust 33

Chapter 7: Transformational Leadership 39

Chapter 8: Partnering and the Future of Work 47

Chapter 9: The Spiritual Aspect – A Holistic View 53

Chapter 10: Creating a Culture 59

Chapter 11: Measuring Success 67

Chapter 12: The Legacy of Partnering 75

Chapter 13: A Path to Collective Transformation 81

About the Author: Zen Benefiel 89

Chapter 1: The Foundations of Partnering

The concept of partnering may seem straightforward—teams working together toward a common goal. But true partnering goes far beyond simple collaboration. It's about fostering a culture of mutual trust, respect, and shared responsibility, where every individual feels valued and aligned with the collective vision. Partnering transforms teams from loosely connected individuals into a cohesive unit, working in harmony to achieve something greater than the sum of their parts. This chapter will explore the foundational principles of partnering, showing how this approach can revolutionize the way we work together.

At its core, partnering is built on three key pillars: **open communication, mutual trust, and shared accountability**. When these elements are in place, teams are empowered to innovate, solve problems together, and move toward a common objective with greater speed and efficiency. But achieving true partnering requires more than just a good intention; it demands commitment, structure, and a willingness to move beyond traditional hierarchies.

1.1 Open Communication: The Bedrock of Trust

In any team or project, communication is critical. It's the foundation on which all other aspects of partnering rest. Without clear, open channels of communication, misunderstandings can arise, conflicts can escalate, and team members can become disconnected from the overall mission. But partnering takes communication to the next level. It's not just about sharing information—it's about creating a space where team members feel safe to express their ideas, concerns, and feedback without fear of judgment or retribution.

In my own experience, whether managing complex aerospace projects or coordinating large-scale events, communication has always been the most important factor in determining success or failure. When teams operate in environments where communication flows freely, creativity and collaboration naturally follow. Issues are addressed quickly, and team members are more willing to step up and contribute to solutions. In a partnering environment, communication is not just about logistics or updates—it's about engaging in meaningful dialogue that builds trust and strengthens relationships.

To foster open communication, it's essential to create structures that encourage dialogue from all levels of the team. This includes regular check-ins, transparent reporting, and open forums for discussing challenges and opportunities. Leaders, especially, must model effective communication by being approachable, clear, and consistent. But more importantly, they must listen—truly listen—to their teams. When leaders demonstrate that they value input from all members, a culture of openness naturally develops, allowing everyone to contribute fully.

1.2 Mutual Trust: The Glue That Holds Teams Together

Trust is often cited as one of the most important factors in any successful relationship, and it's no different when it comes to partnering. In fact, trust is the glue that holds teams together, particularly in high-stakes environments where stress and pressure can cause friction. Trust allows teams to operate smoothly, knowing that each member is reliable, competent, and aligned with the shared goals of the project.

In traditional hierarchical structures, trust can sometimes be undermined by power dynamics. Team members may hesitate to share concerns or innovative ideas if they fear repercussions. Partnering, however, eliminates this fear by flattening the hierarchy and promoting a culture where all contributions are valued equally. It encourages collaboration rather than competition, and cooperation rather than control.

Building trust takes time and consistent effort. It's established through actions that demonstrate integrity, reliability, and respect. Leaders play a key role here—they must be transparent, fair, and accountable, leading by example and showing that they trust their teams to carry out the work. When leaders trust their teams, teams respond by trusting each other, creating a positive feedback loop that strengthens the entire group.

Trust is also about vulnerability—about being open with one another and acknowledging when help is needed or when mistakes are made. In a partnering environment, admitting to a mistake isn't seen as a failure but as an opportunity to learn and grow. When team members feel comfortable being vulnerable, they are more likely to take risks, share innovative ideas, and work together to overcome obstacles.

1.3 Shared Accountability: Owning the Outcome Together

One of the key distinctions between partnering and more traditional work structures is the concept of shared accountability. In many organizations, accountability is often delegated—leaders are responsible for outcomes, while team members are responsible for their specific tasks. In partnering, however, accountability is a collective responsibility. Every member of the team, from top to bottom, shares in the success or failure of the project.

This shift in perspective has a profound impact on how teams operate. When everyone feels accountable for the overall outcome, they are more likely to take ownership of their roles and go above and beyond to ensure the project's success. Shared accountability fosters a sense of unity and commitment that is hard to replicate in more hierarchical structures.

In my experience working with Team Partnering LLC, we've seen firsthand how shared accountability can transform project dynamics. Teams that adopt a partnering approach are more proactive, more engaged, and more invested in the long-term success of the project. When problems arise, they are dealt with collectively, and solutions are developed through collaboration, rather than finger-pointing or blame.

To cultivate shared accountability, it's important to clearly define roles and expectations while also emphasizing the collective nature of the work.

Everyone must understand how their individual contributions impact the overall project and feel empowered to take ownership of their tasks. Leaders must also reinforce the idea that success is a shared accomplishment, and setbacks are a shared responsibility.

1.4 The Power of Synergy: Coagulating Possibilities

When open communication, mutual trust, and shared accountability come together, something remarkable happens—synergy. Synergy is the idea that the whole is greater than the sum of its parts. In a partnering environment, individual talents and perspectives combine to create solutions that none of the team members could have developed on their own. This is where true innovation and progress happen.

Synergy is more than just teamwork; it's the result of a deeply aligned, highly communicative, and fully accountable team working together in harmony. It's the creative spark that ignites when diverse ideas, perspectives, and experiences come together in an open, trusting environment. Synergy is what makes partnering so powerful—it turns ordinary teams into extraordinary ones, capable of achieving incredible things.

As we move forward in this book, we'll explore how these foundational principles of partnering—open communication, mutual trust, shared accountability, and synergy—can be applied to various work environments, from small teams to large-scale projects. We'll look at real-world examples and practical strategies for implementing partnering practices in your own work, and how embracing this approach can lead to greater success, harmony, and fulfillment for everyone involved.

In the following chapters, we'll build on these foundations and explore how partnering can lead to conflict resolution, stronger leadership, and a more harmonious work culture. Let's continue this journey of discovery and see how partnering can transform not only your projects but your entire approach to collaboration.

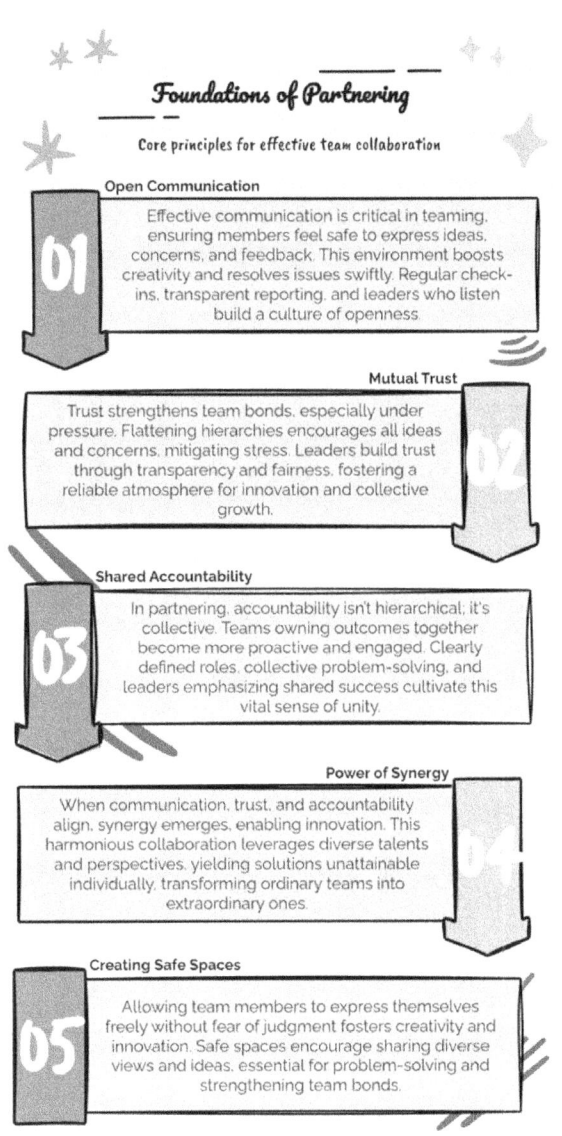

Chapter 2: Solutions – A New Approach

Partnering, in its essence, is about creating an environment where collaboration flourishes, conflicts are resolved early, and all stakeholders are aligned toward a common goal. In this chapter, we will delve into the model I co-created with Team Partnering LLC and how it reshapes the way teams and organizations approach complex projects. By integrating structured collaboration and communication into project planning from the outset, Team Partnering LLC sets the stage for smoother execution, better outcomes, and more harmonious work environments.

Team Partnering LLC was born out of a need to address the growing complexities of large-scale projects—particularly in industries like construction, where multiple stakeholders, tight deadlines, and large budgets make collaboration essential. I had seen firsthand how the lack of communication or misaligned expectations could derail projects, create friction, and waste valuable resources. Our goal was simple: to create a structured process that ensures everyone is aligned, communicating effectively, and working together to achieve the best possible outcome.

2.1 The Partnering Process: A Blueprint for Success

The success of any project hinges on how well the team works together from the very beginning. The partnering process we use at Team Partnering LLC involves a structured, facilitated approach to ensure that all stakeholders are on the same page. From project owners to contractors, architects, and subcontractors, each party has a voice, and their expectations and concerns are addressed upfront. This not only helps align goals but also sets the tone for the entire project.

Partnering begins with a facilitated meeting where we bring all key stakeholders together. This is a critical step because it establishes a baseline for open communication, mutual trust, and shared accountability. In this session, we create a collaborative environment that encourages honest dialogue. We discuss project goals, identify potential challenges, and most importantly, we clarify everyone's roles and responsibilities. This early alignment is essential to prevent misunderstandings or miscommunication later in the project.

The partnering process also includes regular check-ins throughout the project's lifecycle. These check-ins allow the team to assess progress, address any emerging issues, and make adjustments if necessary. It's a proactive approach that ensures issues are addressed before they escalate into bigger problems. These consistent touchpoints keep everyone accountable and foster a continuous flow of communication, which is critical for long-term success.

2.2 Defining Roles and Expectations: The Key to Preventing Conflict

One of the most common sources of conflict in any project is unclear or misaligned expectations. When team members are not sure what is expected of them or if their goals differ from those of their colleagues, tensions can arise. At Team Partnering LLC, we place a heavy emphasis on defining clear roles and expectations from the very start.

In our initial partnering sessions, we work with all parties to establish what success looks like for each stakeholder and how it aligns with the project's overall objectives. This creates a shared understanding of what each team member is responsible for and how their contributions fit into the larger picture. Everyone walks away knowing exactly what is expected of them and what they can expect from others, reducing the likelihood of misunderstandings down the line.

Defining roles also helps mitigate one of the biggest issues in complex projects: scope creep. When stakeholders are unclear about their specific roles, they may take on tasks that fall outside their scope, leading to inefficiencies and confusion. By clearly defining the boundaries of each role, we ensure that everyone stays focused on their areas of expertise while remaining aligned with the overall project goals.

2.3 Creating a Collaborative Environment: Fostering Innovation and Problem-Solving

One of the most powerful outcomes of the partnering process is the creation of a collaborative environment where team members feel empowered to contribute their ideas and solutions. When teams are siloed or operate under a hierarchical structure, innovation can be stifled. People may feel reluctant to speak up or offer suggestions if they believe it's not their place or if they fear rejection. Partnering breaks down these barriers.

At Team Partnering LLC, we encourage an environment of open collaboration where every voice is heard, and all ideas are welcome. This fosters a culture of innovation where team members feel comfortable sharing their perspectives, knowing that their input is valued. It's in these moments of collaboration that creative solutions to complex problems often emerge. By promoting a culture where innovation is encouraged, we not only improve project outcomes but also create a more satisfying work environment for everyone involved.

Additionally, this collaborative environment fosters rapid problem-solving. When issues arise—whether they are technical challenges, timeline adjustments, or interpersonal conflicts—teams are more likely to address them constructively when they've established a strong foundation of trust and open communication. Problems are seen as opportunities for collaboration rather than points of contention.

2.4 Anticipating and Resolving Conflicts Early

No project is without its challenges, and even with the best planning, conflicts will inevitably arise. What sets successful projects apart from others is how these conflicts are handled. The partnering process is designed to anticipate potential conflicts early on and create mechanisms for resolving them before they become larger issues.

One of the key tools we use at Team Partnering LLC is the development of a conflict resolution plan during the initial partnering session. We identify potential areas of friction—whether they be differences in priorities, scheduling conflicts, or budget concerns—and outline a clear process for addressing them. This proactive approach allows teams to tackle issues head-on rather than letting them fester and escalate.

The conflict resolution plan is paired with regular communication touchpoints throughout the project, ensuring that minor concerns are addressed early before they turn into major roadblocks. This approach fosters a culture of transparency where team members feel comfortable raising concerns, knowing that they will be dealt with constructively and respectfully.

2.5 The Results: Efficiency, Satisfaction, and Success

The results of implementing the partnering approach at Team Partnering LLC speak for themselves. Projects that embrace partnering are completed more efficiently, with fewer delays, budget overruns, and conflicts. Teams report higher satisfaction, both in terms of their work and their relationships with colleagues and stakeholders. Most importantly, the project's end result is often superior, with goals met or exceeded and stakeholders satisfied with the process and outcomes.

Partnering doesn't just deliver results—it transforms the way teams work together. By fostering a culture of collaboration, trust, and shared responsibility, partnering creates an environment where everyone can contribute their best and feel invested in the success of the project. It's more than just a strategy for managing projects; it's a philosophy for building better teams, better outcomes, and ultimately, better work environments.

As we continue through the following chapters, we'll explore how partnering principles can be applied across various industries and work environments. We'll dive deeper into how partnering fosters personal and organizational growth, builds stronger leaders, and creates harmony in both professional and personal life. The journey of partnering is one of continuous learning, and I'm excited to share the insights and strategies that will help you make partnering a cornerstone of your success.

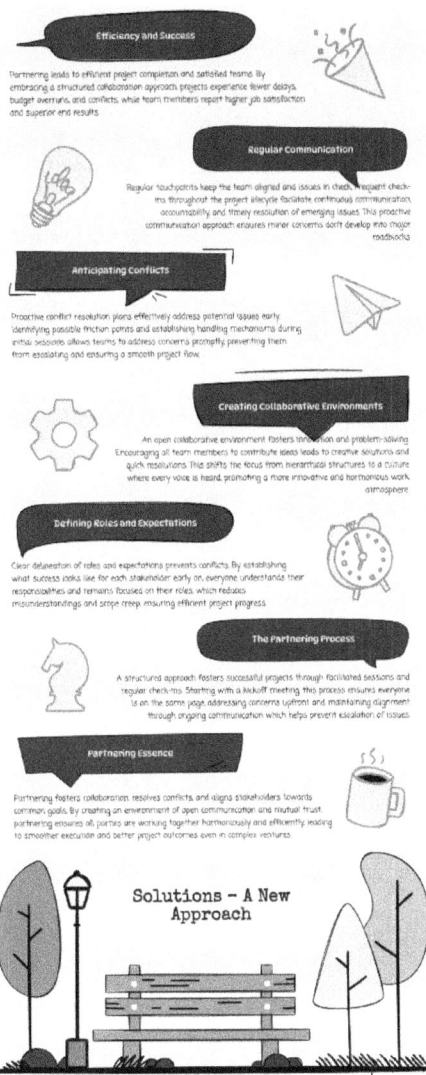

Chapter 3: Navigating Holistic Growth

Partnering is not just a set of strategies for managing projects or building teams—it's a philosophy that can transform both personal and collective growth. As we've explored the principles of partnering and its applications in team dynamics, we begin to see that the benefits extend far beyond the workplace. When approached holistically, partnering becomes a powerful tool for aligning our internal world with our external responsibilities. It invites us to grow not only as team members or leaders but as individuals seeking harmony within ourselves and with those around us.

In this chapter, we will explore how the principles of partnering can be applied to holistic personal growth. By combining elements of collaboration, trust, accountability, and open communication, partnering can foster deeper connections between our personal aspirations and professional goals. We'll discuss the role of self-awareness, emotional intelligence, and empathetic leadership in creating environments where both personal and collective growth thrive. Through real-world examples and insights from my holistic coaching practices, we will see how partnering can help us navigate life's complexities with greater ease, authenticity, and fulfillment.

3.1 Partnering with Yourself: The Foundation of Holistic Growth

Before we can effectively partner with others, we must first learn to partner with ourselves. This may sound like a strange concept at first, but it's essential. Partnering with yourself means cultivating self-awareness, understanding your strengths and weaknesses, and being honest with yourself about your goals, values, and motivations. It involves taking responsibility for your own growth and creating a plan to achieve it, just as you would in any successful partnership.

Self-partnering requires a deep level of introspection and a commitment to personal development. It's about checking in with yourself regularly, just as you would with a project team, to ensure that you're aligned with your goals and moving forward in a way that feels authentic and purposeful. This process of self-reflection helps us build the emotional intelligence necessary to partner effectively with others. By understanding ourselves more fully, we're better equipped to navigate challenges, resolve conflicts, and create harmonious relationships in both our personal and professional lives.

A key aspect of self-partnering is learning to balance ambition with self-care. In a world that often glorifies hustle and productivity, it's easy to lose sight of our own needs. But true growth doesn't come from pushing ourselves to the brink of burnout; it comes from creating space for reflection, renewal, and self-compassion. When we take the time to nurture our physical, mental, and emotional well-being, we are better able to show up as our best selves in our partnerships with others.

3.2 Empathetic Leadership: The Heart of Partnering

In any successful partnership, empathy plays a critical role. Empathy allows us to understand and appreciate the perspectives, needs, and emotions of others. It's the foundation of trust, and it creates the conditions for open, honest communication. In leadership, empathy is the key to building strong, resilient teams where individuals feel valued, supported, and motivated to contribute their best.

Empathetic leadership is more than just a management style—it's a way of being. It requires us to listen actively, show compassion, and respond to the needs of our team members in meaningful ways. This kind of leadership fosters an environment of psychological safety, where people feel comfortable sharing their ideas, challenges, and concerns without fear of judgment or retaliation.

As we explore the principles of partnering, it's important to recognize that empathy doesn't mean sacrificing accountability or standards. Empathetic leaders can still hold their teams to high expectations while creating a supportive, nurturing environment. It's about balancing compassion with responsibility—understanding that people will rise to the occasion when they feel trusted and valued, but also providing the guidance and structure they need to succeed.

Empathy also plays a crucial role in conflict resolution. In any partnership, conflicts are inevitable. But when we approach conflicts with empathy, we're able to see beyond the immediate disagreement and understand the underlying emotions and needs that are driving the conflict. This allows us to address the root cause of the issue, rather than just the surface-level symptoms. In my experience working with teams and individuals, I've seen how empathetic leadership can turn conflicts into opportunities for growth and innovation.

3.3 Emotional Intelligence and Partnering

Emotional intelligence (EQ) is another critical component of holistic growth and partnering. EQ is the ability to recognize, understand, and manage our own emotions, as well as the emotions of others. In the context of partnering, emotional intelligence allows us to navigate complex interpersonal dynamics with grace, composure, and self-awareness.

In teams, high emotional intelligence fosters stronger relationships and better communication. Leaders with high EQ are able to build trust, inspire collaboration, and create an environment where team members feel heard and understood. They're also better equipped to manage stress, stay calm under pressure, and make thoughtful, informed decisions.

But emotional intelligence is not just about managing relationships with others—it's also about managing the relationship we have with ourselves. As we navigate our own growth, we must be aware of the emotions and beliefs that influence our decisions and behaviors. By developing our emotional intelligence, we gain greater insight into our own patterns and motivations, which allows us to make more conscious choices in both our personal and professional lives.

One of the ways we can cultivate emotional intelligence is through mindfulness practices. Mindfulness helps us become more attuned to our thoughts, feelings, and reactions, allowing us to respond to situations with greater clarity and intention. When we bring mindfulness into our partnerships—whether with ourselves or with others—we create space for deeper understanding and more meaningful connections.

3.4 The Synergy of Personal and Collective Growth

One of the most powerful aspects of partnering is the synergy it creates between personal and collective growth. In a true partnership, the success of the individual is inextricably linked to the success of the group. When we invest in our own growth, we bring more to the table in our partnerships with others. Similarly, when we support the growth of those around us, we contribute to the overall success of the team or organization.

This synergy is at the heart of holistic growth. It's about recognizing that our personal development doesn't happen in isolation—it's shaped by our relationships, our work, and our interactions with the world around us. When we approach growth from a holistic perspective, we see that every area of our life is interconnected, and progress in one area can fuel progress in another.

In my holistic coaching practice, I've seen how partnering principles can help individuals unlock their full potential by aligning their personal goals with the goals of their teams and organizations. By fostering open communication, mutual trust, and shared accountability, partnering creates an environment where personal and collective growth thrive side by side.

3.5 Practical Tools for Holistic Partnering

Now that we've explored the concepts of self-partnering, empathetic leadership, and emotional intelligence, let's look at some practical tools for applying these principles in your own life and work:

1. **Self-Reflection Practices**: Regularly take time to check in with yourself—journal, meditate, or engage in activities that help you gain clarity on your goals, values, and emotions.
2. **Active Listening Techniques**: When partnering with others, practice active listening by giving your full attention, asking open-ended questions, and reflecting on what you've heard before responding.
3. **Empathy Mapping**: Use empathy mapping to understand the needs and emotions of your team members. This can help you better navigate conflicts and support their growth.
4. **Emotional Regulation Tools**: Cultivate emotional intelligence by learning techniques for managing stress and regulating emotions, such as deep breathing, visualization, or mindfulness exercises.
5. **Feedback Loops**: Create feedback loops in your personal and professional partnerships to ensure open communication and continuous growth. Regularly ask for and offer constructive feedback to strengthen relationships and improve outcomes.

In the following chapters, we'll explore how these holistic partnering principles can be applied to leadership, conflict resolution, and team dynamics. By fostering both personal and collective growth, we can create partnerships that are not only successful but deeply fulfilling, both professionally and personally. Let's continue this journey toward greater harmony, fulfillment, and success.

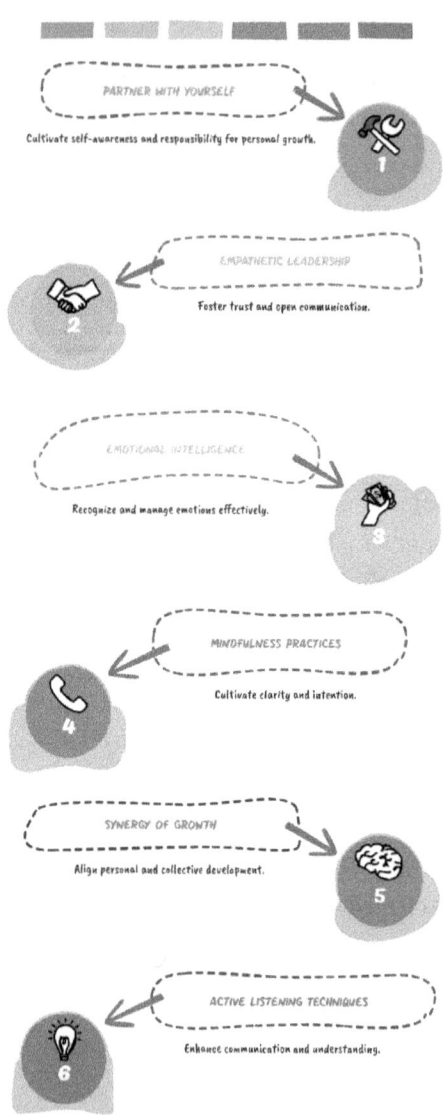

Chapter 4: A Tool for Conflict Resolution

Conflict is an inevitable part of life, especially in environments where diverse ideas, goals, and personalities come together. Whether within families, friendships, or work teams, disagreements and misunderstandings arise, often leading to frustration and division. In many traditional work environments, conflict is seen as a negative force, something to be avoided or suppressed. However, when approached with the right mindset, conflict can actually be a powerful catalyst for growth, innovation, and deeper understanding. This is where partnering steps in as a transformative tool for conflict resolution.

Partnering changes the way we perceive and manage conflict. Instead of viewing disagreements as obstacles, partnering encourages us to see them as opportunities for collaboration and mutual understanding. By fostering open communication, mutual trust, and shared accountability, partnering creates an environment where conflicts can be addressed head-on and resolved constructively. In this chapter, we'll explore how the principles of partnering can be used to resolve conflicts in ways that not only solve immediate issues but strengthen relationships and enhance team dynamics.

4.1 Understanding the Nature of Conflict

Before we can effectively resolve conflict, it's essential to understand what conflict truly is. Conflict arises when two or more parties have differing opinions, needs, or goals. In many cases, these differences are not inherently problematic. In fact, they can lead to creative solutions, new perspectives, and better outcomes—if handled properly. The problem arises when conflicts are ignored, suppressed, or mishandled, allowing tension to build and relationships to deteriorate.

At its core, conflict is a signal that something needs attention. It's a natural part of any dynamic system, whether it's a family, a workplace, or a project team. The key to managing conflict is not to avoid it, but to address it openly and constructively, using it as an opportunity to strengthen connections and find common ground.

Partnering offers a proactive approach to conflict resolution. Rather than waiting for conflicts to escalate, partnering encourages teams to anticipate potential areas of friction and create mechanisms for resolving issues early. This shift from reactive to proactive conflict management can make a profound difference in the way teams function and how individuals relate to one another.

4.2 The Role of Communication in Resolving Conflict

At the heart of every conflict lies communication—or the lack thereof. Many conflicts stem from misunderstandings, miscommunications, or assumptions that haven't been openly discussed. When teams or individuals don't communicate effectively, it's easy for small disagreements to snowball into larger issues. This is why open, honest communication is critical for resolving conflicts.

In the partnering process, communication is not just about conveying information; it's about fostering a dialogue where all parties feel heard and understood. This requires active listening—taking the time to really hear what the other person is saying, without jumping to conclusions or formulating a response before they've finished speaking. It also involves asking clarifying questions to ensure that everyone is on the same page and that no assumptions are being made.

One of the most powerful tools in conflict resolution is **reflective listening**. Reflective listening involves paraphrasing or summarizing what the other person has said to confirm understanding. This technique not only helps clarify the message but also shows the speaker that their perspective is being valued. Reflective listening creates a space for empathy and mutual understanding, which are essential for resolving conflicts constructively.

Additionally, it's important to create a safe environment for communication. In a partnering culture, individuals feel comfortable expressing their concerns and frustrations without fear of retribution or judgment. When people trust that their voices will be heard and their feelings respected, they are more likely to engage in honest dialogue, leading to more productive conflict resolution.

4.3 Shifting from Blame to Accountability

In many traditional conflict scenarios, blame often becomes the dominant theme. People focus on who is at fault, which only deepens the divide and fuels tension. Partnering shifts the focus from blame to accountability. Instead of pointing fingers, partnering encourages all parties to take responsibility for their role in the conflict and work together to find a solution.

Accountability is a cornerstone of the partnering process. It requires individuals to acknowledge their actions, decisions, and contributions—both positive and negative—to the situation. This doesn't mean assigning blame; rather, it means taking ownership of what each person can do to move forward. When everyone takes responsibility for their part in the conflict, it becomes easier to find common ground and work toward a resolution.

One of the most effective ways to foster accountability is through **clear communication of expectations**. By clearly defining roles, responsibilities, and expectations from the outset, teams can minimize misunderstandings and create a foundation for mutual accountability. In the partnering process, we establish this clarity early, during initial project discussions, ensuring that everyone is aligned and understands their contributions to the overall goal.

When conflicts do arise, revisiting these expectations can help clarify where misalignments occurred and how to address them. Rather than focusing on who "messed up," partnering encourages teams to ask, "How can we work together to fix this?" This collaborative mindset transforms conflict from a source of division into a pathway to stronger teamwork.

4.4 Collaborative Problem-Solving: Turning Conflict into Opportunity

One of the most powerful outcomes of partnering is the way it turns conflict into an opportunity for growth and innovation. When teams approach conflict with a partnering mindset, they don't just aim to resolve the issue—they look for ways to use the conflict as a catalyst for creative problem-solving.

Collaborative problem-solving involves bringing all parties together to brainstorm solutions that benefit everyone. It's about moving beyond a zero-sum mindset, where one party "wins" and the other "loses," and instead finding solutions that meet the needs of all involved. This process requires open communication, empathy, and a willingness to consider new perspectives.

In many cases, conflicts arise because people have different ways of approaching a problem. Rather than seeing these differences as obstacles, partnering views them as opportunities for innovation. By combining diverse perspectives and ideas, teams can develop solutions that none of the individuals could have created on their own.

One tool we use in collaborative problem-solving is **brainstorming sessions**. During these sessions, we encourage team members to share their ideas without fear of judgment or criticism. The goal is to generate as many ideas as possible, even if some seem unconventional or far-fetched. Once all ideas are on the table, the team can work together to evaluate them and select the best solution. This process not only resolves the conflict but also strengthens the team's ability to work together in the future.

4.5 Facilitating Difficult Conversations

While some conflicts can be resolved through open dialogue and collaborative problem-solving, others may require more structured facilitation. This is especially true in situations where emotions run high or where long-standing issues have created deep divisions. In these cases, partnering offers a framework for facilitating difficult conversations in a way that promotes understanding and healing.

Facilitating difficult conversations involves creating a safe space where all parties can express their concerns, frustrations, and emotions without fear of escalation. The facilitator's role is to guide the conversation, ensuring that it remains respectful, focused, and productive. This often involves setting ground rules for the conversation, such as allowing each person to speak without interruption and committing to a solution-oriented mindset.

One of the key elements of facilitating difficult conversations is **acknowledgment**. Before diving into solutions, it's important to acknowledge the emotions and experiences of everyone involved. This doesn't mean agreeing with every perspective, but it does mean validating the feelings and concerns that have been expressed. When people feel acknowledged, they are more likely to engage in constructive dialogue and work toward a resolution.

The partnering process is designed to prevent conflicts from escalating to this point by fostering continuous communication and early problem-solving. However, when deeper issues do arise, facilitated conversations can provide the space needed to resolve them in a way that strengthens, rather than weakens, relationships.

4.6 Long-Term Benefits of Conflict Resolution Through Partnering

The long-term benefits of resolving conflicts through partnering extend far beyond the immediate resolution of issues. Teams that use partnering to address conflicts early and constructively build stronger relationships, develop better communication skills, and foster a culture of mutual respect and collaboration. These benefits don't just improve team dynamics—they also lead to more successful projects, higher levels of engagement, and greater satisfaction for all involved.

When conflicts are resolved in a way that strengthens relationships, teams become more resilient. They are better equipped to handle future challenges, adapt to changing circumstances, and maintain a positive, productive work environment. In this sense, partnering isn't just a tool for conflict resolution—it's a foundation for long-term success.

As we continue through this book, we'll explore how partnering principles can be applied to leadership, team dynamics, and the development of high-performing teams. By embracing conflict as an opportunity for growth and innovation, we can create work environments where collaboration thrives, and success is shared by all. Let's move forward together on this journey of discovery, learning how to navigate challenges with grace, wisdom, and a commitment to mutual growth.

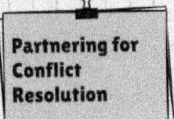

Partnering for Conflict Resolution

1. Understanding Nature of Conflict

Conflicts arise from differing opinions, needs, or goals. Recognizing that conflicts are natural signals for attention, rather than threats, allows teams to address issues openly and constructively, transforming potential obstacles into opportunities for collaboration and stronger relationships.

2. Role of Communication

Effective communication is crucial for conflict resolution. Open, honest dialogue allows parties to understand one another fully, preventing misunderstandings and assumptions. Techniques like reflective listening foster empathy and mutual understanding, crucial elements in resolving conflicts constructively.

3. Shifting from Blame to Accountability

Focus on accountability over blame. Encouraging individuals to take responsibility for their roles in a conflict helps in finding common ground and working toward resolutions. Clear communication of expectations can minimize misunderstandings and create a stronger foundation for mutual accountability.

4. Collaborative Problem-Solving

Transform conflicts into collaboration opportunities. By encouraging teams to brainstorm and evaluate diverse solutions together, conflicts can serve as catalysts for innovation and stronger teamwork, moving from zero-sum outcomes to mutually beneficial solutions.

5. Facilitating Difficult Conversations

Structured conversations helps resolve deeper conflicts. Creating a safe, respectful space for open dialogue allows all parties to express concerns without escalation, promoting understanding and healing. Acknowledgment of emotions and experiences is key for constructive discussions.

6. Long-Term Benefits

Partnering builds resilient teams. Resolving conflicts constructively enhances team dynamics, fosters mutual respect, and leads to more successful projects. This approach not only addresses immediate issues but also lays the foundation for long-term success and adaptability.

7. Active Listening

Active listening is essential for ensuring that all parties feel heard and understood. By paraphrasing or summarizing the speaker's points, reflective listening can reduce misunderstandings, build trust, and create a more collaborative and empathetic environment for resolving conflicts.

8. Proactive Conflict Management

Anticipate and address conflicts early. Proactively managing conflicts before they escalate can prevent misunderstandings from turning into major issues, leading to a more harmonious and productive team environment. This shift from reactive to proactive management is crucial.

Chapter 5: The Role of Servant Leadership

At the heart of successful partnering is the concept of leadership—not the traditional top-down model where power is concentrated at the top, but rather a model rooted in service. Servant leadership flips the conventional leadership paradigm by emphasizing the leader's role in supporting, empowering, and elevating their team. This type of leadership is perfectly aligned with the principles of partnering, as both prioritize collaboration, trust, and the well-being of every individual in the group.

In this chapter, we will explore the fundamentals of servant leadership and how it seamlessly integrates with the partnering approach. We'll discuss the qualities of servant leaders, the transformative effects they have on teams, and practical ways to adopt servant leadership in your work environment. Through real-life examples and leadership insights, we will see how servant leadership not only improves project outcomes but also fosters a culture of growth, accountability, and fulfillment.

5.1 What is Servant Leadership?

Servant leadership is a philosophy that focuses on serving the needs of others first. In contrast to traditional leadership models, where the leader's primary goal is to manage, control, or direct, the servant leader's main goal is to serve their team, ensuring that each person has what they need to succeed. By empowering and supporting others, the servant leader creates an environment where individuals feel valued and motivated to contribute their best.

Robert K. Greenleaf, who popularized the concept in the 1970s, described servant leadership as a model where "the servant-leader is servant first." This idea is not new—it can be traced back to ancient philosophies and spiritual traditions—but it has gained significant traction in the modern business world as organizations seek more ethical, sustainable, and human-centered leadership approaches.

In the context of partnering, servant leadership enhances collaboration by placing the focus on team members' well-being and growth. Rather than seeking to control outcomes, the servant leader facilitates environments where individuals can thrive and contribute meaningfully to the collective effort. When leadership is based on service, trust naturally builds, relationships strengthen, and the team becomes more cohesive and resilient.

5.2 The Qualities of a Servant Leader

Servant leaders embody a unique set of qualities that distinguish them from more traditional leaders. These qualities not only create a more harmonious work environment but also help teams achieve greater success through genuine collaboration and shared accountability. Here are some of the key qualities of a servant leader:

- **Empathy**: Servant leaders practice empathy by understanding and appreciating the perspectives and emotions of their team members. They listen actively, seek to understand before offering solutions, and prioritize the emotional and psychological well-being of their teams.

- **Humility**: A servant leader does not seek power for its own sake. Instead, they recognize that leadership is a responsibility, not a privilege. Humility allows leaders to admit when they don't have all the answers and encourages them to seek input from others.

- **Vision**: Servant leaders have a clear, inspiring vision for the future, but their focus is on helping their team share and co-create that vision. They guide with purpose while encouraging collective ownership of the goals.

- **Trust**: Servant leaders build and maintain trust through transparency, honesty, and consistent actions. Trust is a critical foundation for any successful team, and servant leaders go out of their way to ensure that trust remains intact, even in difficult situations.

- **Empowerment**: Rather than micromanaging or controlling, servant leaders empower their team members to take ownership of their work. They provide the resources, support, and freedom needed for individuals to grow and thrive within their roles.
- **Commitment to Growth**: A servant leader is deeply invested in the personal and professional growth of their team members. They look for ways to develop the talents and skills of those around them, whether through mentoring, training, or providing opportunities for leadership.

These qualities form the foundation of a servant leadership approach that aligns perfectly with partnering. Servant leaders act as facilitators, ensuring that every individual feels heard, respected, and empowered to contribute to the project's success.

5.3 Servant Leadership and Partnering: A Perfect Fit

Servant leadership and partnering share many of the same values and goals, making them a natural fit for one another. Both approaches focus on collaboration, mutual respect, and the belief that success is a shared responsibility. In partnering, the leader's role is not to control the team but to serve as a guide and support system, helping the group navigate challenges and work toward a common goal.

In the partnering process, leaders create an environment where open communication thrives, conflicts are addressed constructively, and accountability is shared. This mirrors the role of a servant leader, who prioritizes the needs of their team and creates the conditions for effective collaboration. By adopting a servant leadership mindset, project managers and team leaders can enhance the effectiveness of partnering initiatives, ensuring that everyone is aligned and engaged.

Servant leadership also helps foster a sense of ownership among team members. When people feel supported and valued, they are more likely to take responsibility for their contributions and invest in the project's success. This is especially important in partnering, where shared accountability is key. A servant leader creates a sense of shared ownership by empowering individuals to take initiative and encouraging them to bring their unique talents and perspectives to the table.

5.4 Servant Leadership in Action: Real-Life Examples

To better understand how servant leadership enhances partnering, let's look at some real-life examples of servant leadership in action.

In my work with **Team Partnering LLC**, we've seen firsthand how servant leadership transforms project dynamics. On one large-scale construction project, the project manager embraced a servant leadership approach, prioritizing the needs of the subcontractors and ensuring that everyone had the resources and support necessary to meet deadlines. Rather than dictating tasks, the project manager facilitated regular meetings where team members could voice concerns, share ideas, and collaborate on solutions.

As a result, the team operated more smoothly, conflicts were addressed quickly, and the project was completed ahead of schedule. Team members reported feeling more engaged and motivated, and the project's success was attributed in large part to the collaborative, supportive atmosphere created by the servant leadership approach.

Another example comes from my experience in holistic coaching, where leaders who adopt servant leadership principles often see remarkable growth in their teams. By focusing on the personal development of their team members—whether through mentorship, feedback, or providing opportunities for skill-building—servant leaders create a culture of continuous growth. This not only benefits the individual but also enhances the collective capabilities of the team, leading to more innovative solutions and stronger results.

5.5 Practical Steps to Becoming a Servant Leader

If you're interested in adopting a servant leadership approach, there are several practical steps you can take to begin leading with service:

1. **Listen First**: Make it a priority to listen to your team members before offering solutions. Understand their needs, concerns, and perspectives. This builds trust and ensures that your decisions are informed by the collective wisdom of the group.
2. **Empower Others**: Provide your team with the tools, resources, and autonomy they need to succeed. Avoid micromanaging and instead trust your team members to take ownership of their roles.
3. **Lead by Example**: Model the behavior you want to see in your team. Demonstrate humility, empathy, and accountability in your actions, and your team will follow suit.
4. **Encourage Growth**: Invest in the personal and professional development of your team. Provide opportunities for training, mentorship, and leadership, and encourage team members to take on new challenges.
5. **Celebrate Successes Together**: Recognize and celebrate the contributions of your team members. Acknowledge their hard work, and make sure that successes are shared by the entire team, not just leadership.

As we continue through this book, we will explore how servant leadership and partnering principles can transform not only your projects but also your personal growth and relationships. Together, we'll dive deeper into the ways servant leadership fosters harmony, innovation, and long-term success within teams. Let's continue on this journey of discovering how leadership rooted in service can bring out the best in everyone and lead to extraordinary outcomes.

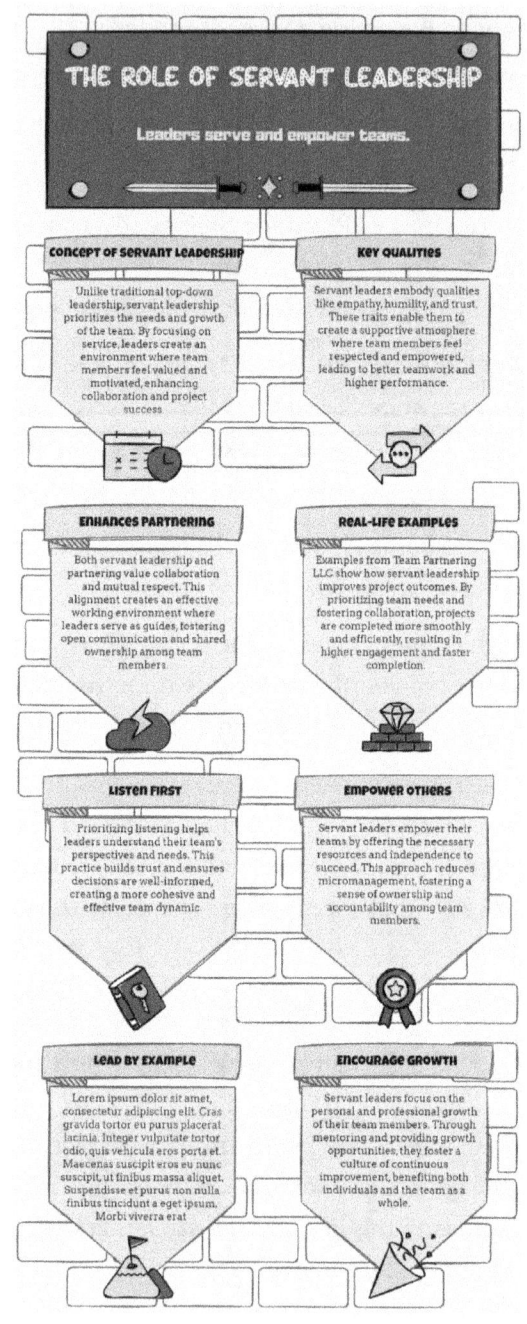

Chapter 6: Breaking Down Silos – Building Trust

In every organization, whether it's a small business or a large corporation, one of the most common barriers to success is the existence of silos. Silos occur when different departments or teams operate independently, often with limited communication and collaboration. While specialization within divisions is important, the lack of cross-functional engagement can lead to inefficiencies, miscommunication, and a fractured organizational culture. Silos prevent information flow, limit innovation, and create bottlenecks in decision-making processes.

In this chapter, we will explore how partnering and servant leadership can break down these silos and foster an environment of collaboration and trust across all levels and divisions. By addressing the root causes of organizational silos and introducing principles of partnering, we can create a culture where departments work together seamlessly, share knowledge openly, and align around common goals. This chapter will highlight how trust, communication, and a shared vision are key to unifying teams and divisions that have traditionally operated in isolation.

6.1 The Problem with Silos: Why They Emerge

Silos are often a byproduct of organizational growth, specialization, or simply an ingrained culture where departments operate independently to achieve their own goals. In large organizations, for example, teams may become so focused on their specific tasks that they lose sight of how their work fits into the bigger picture. They may even feel that protecting their resources or expertise from other departments gives them more control or leverage within the organization.

The danger of silos is that they create barriers to communication and collaboration. When teams don't communicate, they miss opportunities for synergy and innovation. Additionally, when each division operates in isolation, it can lead to misaligned goals, conflicting priorities, and ultimately, inefficiencies that harm the organization as a whole.

These silos also affect the company culture. Employees within different divisions may feel disconnected from the organization's larger mission, leading to disengagement or a sense of competition rather than cooperation. The lack of trust and interaction between departments can foster resentment or misunderstanding, making it difficult to work together effectively when it matters most.

6.2 The Role of Partnering in Breaking Down Silos

The principles of partnering provide a powerful framework for breaking down these silos and fostering a more integrated, collaborative environment. At the core of partnering is the idea of shared responsibility, where each individual or department recognizes that their success is directly tied to the success of the entire organization. This mindset shift encourages teams to look beyond their immediate goals and priorities and work toward the collective good of the company.

One of the first steps in breaking down silos is creating opportunities for departments to communicate and collaborate regularly. In a partnering environment, leaders facilitate meetings or workshops where teams from different divisions can come together, share information, and align on overarching goals. These meetings foster open dialogue, build relationships, and create a sense of shared purpose.

Another critical element of partnering is **transparency**. When teams are siloed, information often becomes guarded or compartmentalized, leading to gaps in understanding. By promoting transparency across divisions, partnering ensures that everyone has access to the information they need to make informed decisions. This open flow of information helps prevent miscommunication, duplication of efforts, and unnecessary conflicts.

For partnering to work effectively, it's important to break down not just organizational silos, but also **mental silos**—the mindset that one department's work is more important than another's. This requires a cultural shift that values the contributions of every team and promotes equality in decision-making. When individuals feel that their work is valued and that they are part of a larger whole, they are more likely to collaborate with others and contribute to the organization's broader mission.

6.3 Trust as the Foundation for Cross-Division Collaboration

Trust is a fundamental element in breaking down silos. Without trust, departments may hesitate to share information, collaborate on projects, or even communicate openly. However, when trust is established, teams become more willing to work together, exchange ideas, and support one another's efforts.

Building trust across divisions requires a deliberate effort from leadership. Leaders must model trust-building behaviors, such as transparency, consistency, and empathy. By being open about their own goals and challenges, leaders can encourage the same openness among their teams. Additionally, trust-building requires patience and persistence—trust doesn't happen overnight, but it can be cultivated through small, consistent actions over time.

One of the most effective ways to build trust is through **shared successes**. When teams from different departments come together to achieve a common goal, it reinforces the idea that collaboration leads to better outcomes. These shared successes should be celebrated publicly, highlighting the contributions of all involved and demonstrating that working together benefits everyone.

In some cases, it may be necessary to **facilitate trust-building exercises** or workshops. These activities allow team members to get to know one another on a deeper level, break down preconceived notions, and develop mutual respect. By creating opportunities for cross-division relationships to form, organizations can lay the groundwork for more effective collaboration moving forward.

6.4 The Power of Cross-Functional Teams

Cross-functional teams are a powerful tool for breaking down silos and fostering collaboration. In a traditional siloed environment, departments are often isolated, focusing only on their immediate objectives. However, by creating cross-functional teams that bring together members from different departments, organizations can tap into a wealth of diverse perspectives, skills, and experiences.

Cross-functional teams encourage departments to work together on projects that require input from multiple areas of expertise. For example, a product development team might include members from engineering, marketing, finance, and customer support. By working together, these team members gain a better understanding of how their work fits into the broader project and how they can support one another in achieving shared goals.

Partnering within cross-functional teams also leads to **innovation**. When diverse minds come together, they are more likely to develop creative solutions to complex problems. The combination of different viewpoints, knowledge bases, and skill sets creates a fertile ground for new ideas to emerge. This innovation would be impossible in a siloed environment, where teams only interact within their own bubble.

For cross-functional teams to succeed, it's essential to establish clear goals, roles, and communication channels. Leaders must ensure that team members have a shared understanding of what they are working toward and how they will achieve it. Regular check-ins, open feedback loops, and shared accountability are all crucial elements of maintaining an effective cross-functional team.

6.5 Aligning Teams Around a Shared Vision

One of the most important aspects of breaking down silos is aligning all teams around a shared vision. When divisions are siloed, they often operate with different goals or priorities. This misalignment can create tension or confusion and may lead to projects that don't fully support the organization's overarching mission.

Partnering provides a way to realign teams by focusing on a shared vision that everyone can get behind. This vision serves as a guiding star, ensuring that all departments are working toward the same ultimate goals, even if their day-to-day tasks differ. Leaders play a key role in communicating this vision clearly and consistently, making sure that it resonates with every team member.

In addition to a shared vision, **mutual accountability** is essential for aligning teams. Partnering emphasizes shared responsibility, meaning that every department is accountable not only for their own success but also for the success of the entire organization. By promoting this culture of mutual accountability, leaders can ensure that all teams stay aligned and work together harmoniously.

6.6 Sustaining Collaboration Beyond Initial Success

While breaking down silos and fostering collaboration is a major achievement, the challenge doesn't end there. Organizations must work to sustain these collaborative efforts long-term, even after initial successes have been achieved. Partnering is not a one-time fix; it's an ongoing process that requires consistent attention and effort.

Leaders should continue to facilitate opportunities for cross-division communication, collaboration, and relationship-building. Regularly scheduled meetings, collaborative projects, and team-building activities can help keep the momentum going and prevent teams from slipping back into siloed behaviors.

Additionally, organizations must be vigilant about maintaining the **culture of trust** and **shared accountability**. This means recognizing and celebrating team successes, addressing conflicts quickly and constructively, and ensuring that transparency and open communication remain core values.

Breaking down silos is one of the most transformative things an organization can do to improve communication, foster innovation, and drive success. By integrating partnering principles, organizations can create an environment where teams collaborate freely, share knowledge openly, and trust one another to work toward shared goals. In the following chapters, we'll continue to explore how these principles of partnering can lead to more cohesive teams, better project outcomes, and a culture of collaboration that fuels long-term success. Let's continue on this journey to creating organizations where collaboration and trust are the cornerstones of everything we do.

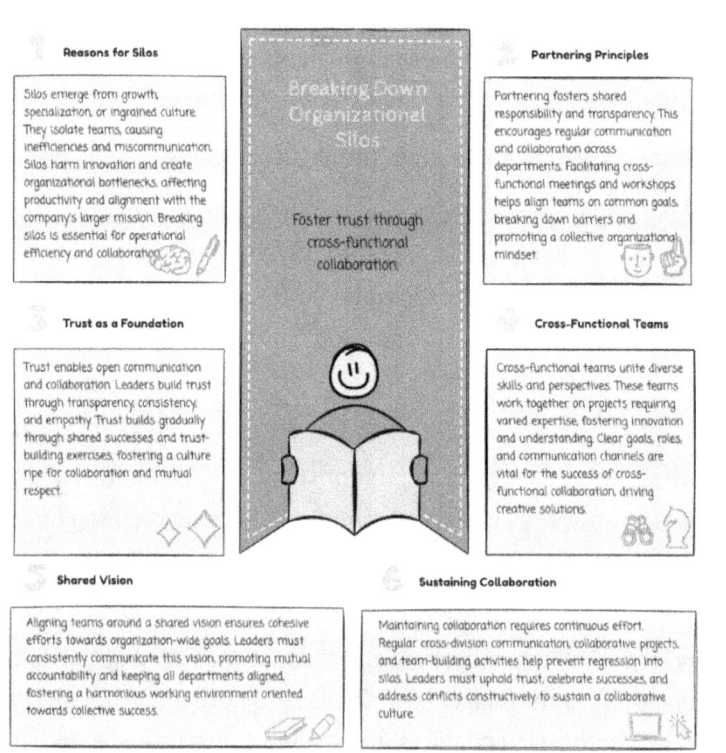

Chapter 7: Transformational Leadership

From Manager to Facilitator

Leadership is evolving. In today's dynamic work environment, the traditional role of a manager—focused on directing, controlling, and overseeing—no longer aligns with the needs of modern teams. The complexity and interconnectedness of today's projects demand a different kind of leadership: one that empowers, supports, and facilitates collaboration. This shift from manager to facilitator is a critical component of partnering, where the leader's role is not to command but to create conditions for success.

In this chapter, we'll explore the concept of transformational leadership and how it complements the partnering approach. Transformational leaders inspire and motivate their teams by focusing on personal and professional growth, fostering a sense of shared purpose, and creating an environment where innovation and collaboration thrive. We'll discuss the qualities of transformational leaders, the impact they have on teams, and practical strategies for shifting from a traditional management style to a facilitative leadership approach.

7.1 The Shift from Manager to Facilitator

Traditionally, managers have been seen as the "boss"—the person in charge, responsible for making decisions, delegating tasks, and ensuring that work is completed on time. This command-and-control approach worked well in hierarchical, rigid structures where roles were clearly defined, and success was measured by adherence to processes. However, in today's world of fast-moving projects, cross-functional teams, and rapid innovation, this model often stifles creativity and limits the potential for collaboration.

The role of a facilitator, on the other hand, is fundamentally different. A facilitator is not there to control every aspect of the project but to support the team in reaching its full potential. Facilitators guide the process, ensure that communication flows smoothly, and create an environment where team members feel empowered to contribute their ideas and expertise. In this sense, a transformational leader serves as a facilitator, focused on bringing out the best in their team rather than micromanaging tasks.

This shift from manager to facilitator involves a fundamental change in mindset. It requires leaders to let go of the need to control every detail and instead trust their teams to take ownership of their work. It also requires a high level of emotional intelligence, empathy, and the ability to create psychological safety—an environment where team members feel comfortable taking risks, sharing ideas, and learning from mistakes.

7.2 The Qualities of a Transformational Leader

Transformational leaders possess a unique set of qualities that distinguish them from more traditional, directive leaders. These qualities enable them to create a culture of trust, innovation, and shared accountability, all of which are essential for successful partnering. Here are some of the key qualities of transformational leaders:

- **Visionary**: Transformational leaders have a clear, compelling vision for the future, and they inspire their teams to work toward that vision. They are not only focused on immediate tasks but also on how their work contributes to the bigger picture. They help their teams see beyond the day-to-day to understand the larger purpose of their efforts.

- **Empowering**: Rather than controlling every decision, transformational leaders empower their team members to take ownership of their work. They provide the resources and support needed for individuals to thrive, while also giving them the autonomy to make decisions and solve problems. This empowerment fosters a sense of responsibility and accountability within the team.

- **Inspirational**: Transformational leaders are skilled at motivating their teams through encouragement and positive reinforcement. They understand that people perform at their best when they feel inspired, engaged, and valued. By recognizing and celebrating their team's achievements, transformational leaders foster a culture of continuous improvement and high morale.

- **Adaptable**: In today's fast-paced work environment, adaptability is crucial. Transformational leaders are flexible and open to change, and they encourage their teams to embrace new ideas, technologies, and ways of working. They recognize that change is inevitable and view it as an opportunity for growth rather than a threat.
- **Collaborative**: Collaboration is at the heart of transformational leadership. These leaders understand that the best solutions come from diverse perspectives, and they actively promote teamwork and cross-functional collaboration. They facilitate open dialogue, encourage idea-sharing, and create an environment where all voices are heard.
- **Emotional Intelligence**: Transformational leaders are emotionally intelligent, meaning they are attuned to the emotions and needs of their team members. They are empathetic, approachable, and skilled at managing interpersonal dynamics. This emotional intelligence allows them to build strong, trusting relationships with their teams.

7.3 Transformational Leadership in the Partnering Process

The principles of transformational leadership align perfectly with the partnering process. Partnering is all about fostering collaboration, building trust, and ensuring that every team member feels empowered to contribute to the project's success. Transformational leaders create the conditions necessary for partnering to thrive by focusing on the growth and development of their team members and facilitating open communication and shared accountability.

In a partnering environment, the leader's role is not to dictate tasks but to guide the process. This involves setting clear goals, ensuring that everyone is aligned around the project's vision, and creating space for collaboration. Transformational leaders do this by asking questions, encouraging dialogue, and removing obstacles that prevent the team from working effectively.

Transformational leaders also play a critical role in **resolving conflicts** within the partnering process. When disagreements arise, they don't rush to impose solutions; instead, they facilitate discussions that allow the team to find common ground and develop their own solutions. By fostering a culture of trust and open communication, transformational leaders ensure that conflicts are addressed constructively, rather than becoming a source of tension or division.

7.4 The Impact of Transformational Leadership on Team Dynamics

Transformational leadership has a profound impact on team dynamics. When leaders adopt a facilitative approach, teams become more cohesive, engaged, and innovative. This is because transformational leaders create an environment where individuals feel valued, supported, and motivated to do their best work.

One of the key benefits of transformational leadership is that it encourages **personal and professional growth**. By empowering team members to take ownership of their roles, transformational leaders help individuals develop new skills, build confidence, and take on leadership responsibilities of their own. This growth not only benefits the individual but also strengthens the overall capabilities of the team.

Transformational leadership also enhances **collaboration**. When leaders foster a culture of openness and trust, team members are more likely to share ideas, seek input from others, and work together to solve problems. This collaborative dynamic leads to better decision-making, more creative solutions, and higher levels of engagement and satisfaction within the team.

Finally, transformational leadership leads to **greater accountability**. When individuals are empowered and trusted to take ownership of their work, they naturally feel a greater sense of responsibility for the project's success. This shared accountability is a cornerstone of the partnering process, where success is seen as a collective achievement rather than the result of one individual's efforts.

7.5 Practical Steps to Becoming a Transformational Leader

If you're ready to transition from a traditional management style to transformational leadership, there are several practical steps you can take to begin facilitating rather than directing your team:

1. **Develop a Vision**: Start by developing a clear, compelling vision for your team or project. This vision should be inspiring and provide a sense of purpose that aligns with the team's values and goals. Communicate this vision clearly and regularly, ensuring that every team member understands how their work contributes to the bigger picture.

2. **Empower Your Team**: Trust your team members to take ownership of their work. Provide them with the resources, support, and autonomy they need to succeed. Encourage them to make decisions, take initiative, and solve problems without waiting for your approval.

3. **Foster Open Communication**: Create an environment where open communication is encouraged and valued. Facilitate regular check-ins, feedback loops, and opportunities for team members to share their ideas and concerns. Practice active listening and ensure that all voices are heard.

4. **Inspire and Motivate**: Use positive reinforcement to inspire and motivate your team. Recognize their achievements, celebrate their successes, and provide constructive feedback that helps them grow.

Lead by example, demonstrating the values and behaviors you want to see in your team.

5. **Adapt to Change**: Be open to change and encourage your team to embrace new ideas and approaches. View challenges as opportunities for growth and innovation, and model a mindset of adaptability and continuous improvement.

Transformational leadership is more than a management style—it's a philosophy of leadership that prioritizes the growth, empowerment, and collaboration of your team. By shifting from a traditional manager to a facilitator, you can create an environment where partnering thrives, innovation flourishes, and success is shared by all. In the next chapter, we'll explore how these principles of transformational leadership can be applied across industries and projects, showing how facilitative leadership can transform not only your team but your entire organization. Let's continue on this journey toward creating leaders who inspire, empower, and elevate those around them.

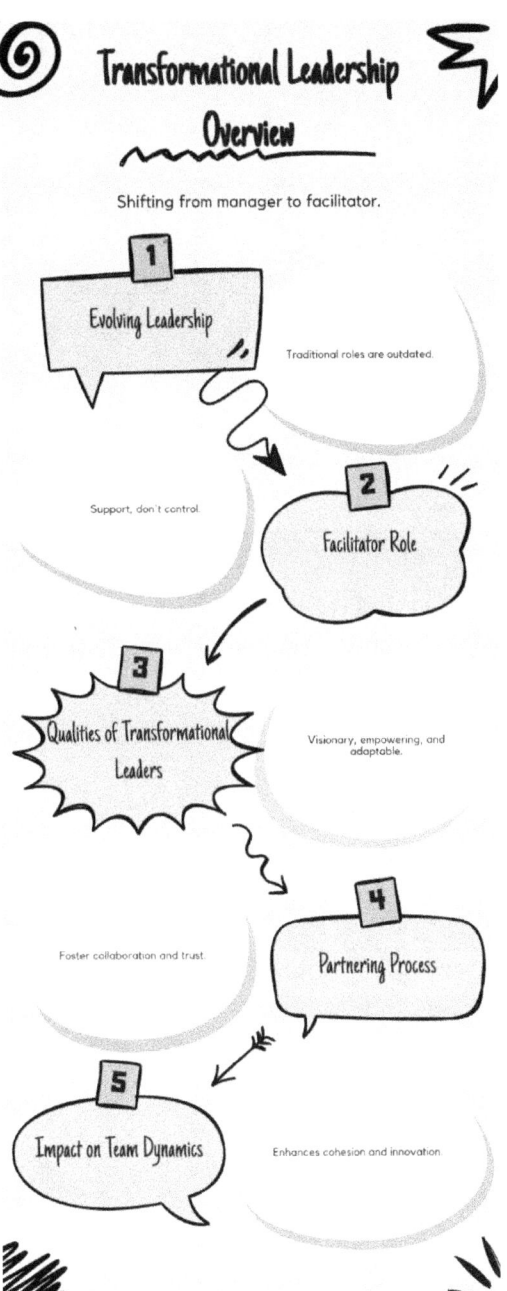

Chapter 8: Partnering and the Future of Work

The future of work is evolving at a pace we've never seen before. Advances in technology, the rise of remote work, the demand for flexible schedules, and the push for more inclusive and diverse workplaces are reshaping how we approach work across all industries. Traditional models of leadership and teamwork are being challenged, and organizations are recognizing the need for more adaptive, collaborative, and human-centered approaches.

In this rapidly changing landscape, partnering offers a powerful solution for navigating the future of work. As teams become more distributed and cross-functional, and as the nature of work itself becomes more complex, the principles of partnering—collaboration, trust, open communication, and shared accountability—are essential for achieving long-term success. In this chapter, we'll explore how partnering principles can be adapted to the future of work, with a focus on remote teams, global collaboration, and the integration of technology. We'll also discuss how partnering fosters innovation and inclusion in increasingly diverse work environments.

8.1 The Rise of Remote and Distributed Teams

One of the most significant shifts in the future of work is the rise of remote and distributed teams. The COVID-19 pandemic accelerated the adoption of remote work, and many organizations have embraced it as a long-term strategy. While remote work offers flexibility and access to global talent, it also presents unique challenges—particularly around communication, collaboration, and maintaining team cohesion.

In a remote environment, the lack of face-to-face interaction can lead to misunderstandings, isolation, and difficulty building trust. However, the principles of partnering provide a framework for overcoming these challenges. By emphasizing open communication, transparency, and regular check-ins, partnering ensures that remote teams stay aligned and connected, even when they are geographically dispersed.

One of the key strategies for partnering with remote teams is to **foster strong communication channels**. In a remote setting, communication needs to be intentional and frequent. Leaders should establish regular team meetings, virtual check-ins, and open forums where team members can share updates, ask questions, and discuss challenges. Video conferencing, messaging apps, and project management tools can facilitate this communication, but the key is to ensure that every team member feels heard and included.

Additionally, partnering encourages **relationship-building** among remote team members. In a traditional office setting, informal conversations and face-to-face interactions help build trust and rapport. In a remote environment, these opportunities are more limited, so it's important to create intentional spaces for connection. Virtual team-building activities, social hours, and informal check-ins can help remote workers build relationships and feel more connected to the team.

8.2 Global Collaboration and Cross-Cultural Partnering

As remote work becomes more prevalent, so does global collaboration. Teams are increasingly composed of individuals from different countries, cultures, and backgrounds, bringing a wealth of diverse perspectives to the table. While this diversity can drive innovation and creativity, it also requires a thoughtful approach to communication and collaboration.

In global teams, cultural differences can affect everything from communication styles to decision-making processes. Partnering principles help bridge these cultural gaps by emphasizing empathy, active listening, and mutual respect. Leaders and team members alike must be aware of and sensitive to cultural differences, ensuring that every voice is heard and valued.

One of the most important aspects of global partnering is **cultural intelligence**—the ability to recognize, understand, and adapt to cultural differences. Partnering encourages teams to engage in open discussions about their cultural norms and expectations, fostering a deeper understanding of each team member's background and perspective. This cultural awareness creates a more inclusive environment where diversity is celebrated, and collaboration flourishes.

Another key element of global partnering is the creation of **shared goals and values**. While team members may come from different cultural backgrounds, they can unite around a common purpose. Leaders play a crucial role in communicating the team's shared vision and ensuring that every team member feels a sense of ownership and responsibility for achieving the group's goals.

8.3 Integrating Technology into Partnering

Technology plays a central role in the future of work, and its integration into the partnering process is essential for success. From project management software to virtual collaboration tools, technology has the potential to enhance communication, streamline workflows, and improve overall efficiency. However, technology is only effective when it is used in alignment with the core principles of partnering.

One of the most important aspects of integrating technology into partnering is **transparency**. In distributed teams, technology can provide real-time visibility into project progress, allowing team members to stay informed and engaged. Tools like shared calendars, task management systems, and collaborative document platforms enable teams to track their work, share updates, and hold each other accountable. By promoting transparency, these tools help ensure that everyone is on the same page and working toward a common goal.

However, it's important to remember that technology should never replace **human connection**. While digital tools can enhance communication and efficiency, they cannot fully replicate the benefits of face-to-face interaction. Leaders should be mindful of this balance and ensure that technology is used to support, rather than hinder, meaningful collaboration. Video calls, for example, can help replicate the nuances of in-person communication, while regular one-on-one check-ins can help maintain personal connections between team members.

Another consideration when integrating technology into partnering is the need for **digital literacy**. As new tools and platforms emerge, it's important to ensure that all team members are comfortable and proficient in using them. Partnering encourages leaders to provide training and support to help team members navigate the technology they use, ensuring that no one is left behind in the digital transformation.

8.4 Fostering Innovation Through Partnering

The future of work is characterized by rapid innovation, and partnering provides a fertile ground for creativity and problem-solving. By bringing together diverse perspectives, encouraging open communication, and fostering a culture of trust, partnering enables teams to develop innovative solutions to complex challenges.

In many organizations, innovation is stifled by rigid hierarchies and siloed departments. Partnering breaks down these barriers by promoting cross-functional collaboration and empowering team members to contribute their ideas freely. In a partnering environment, every team member is encouraged to share their insights, regardless of their role or seniority. This inclusive approach not only leads to more creative solutions but also ensures that everyone feels a sense of ownership over the project's success.

Innovation thrives when teams feel safe to take risks and experiment with new ideas. In a partnering culture, **psychological safety** is a priority—team members know that they can propose new approaches or challenge the status quo without fear of punishment or ridicule. Leaders play a critical role in fostering this environment by modeling openness to new ideas and encouraging experimentation.

Additionally, partnering emphasizes **iterative problem-solving**. Rather than waiting for a perfect solution to emerge, teams in a partnering environment are encouraged to test and refine their ideas through continuous feedback and collaboration. This iterative approach allows teams to adapt quickly to changing circumstances and make improvements along the way.

8.5 Inclusion and Diversity in the Future of Work

As workplaces become more diverse, the need for inclusion is greater than ever. Partnering provides a framework for fostering inclusion by creating a culture where every team member feels valued, respected, and empowered to contribute. By emphasizing empathy, active listening, and shared accountability, partnering ensures that diverse perspectives are not only welcomed but actively sought out.

In the future of work, **inclusion** is about more than simply having a diverse workforce—it's about creating an environment where everyone feels they belong. Partnering helps create this environment by promoting **equal participation** in decision-making processes. Leaders in a partnering environment ensure that all voices are heard and that decisions are made collaboratively, with input from a range of perspectives.

Partnering also helps combat unconscious bias, which can prevent diverse team members from fully contributing. By encouraging open communication and transparency, partnering brings biases to the surface and provides opportunities for dialogue and learning. This commitment to inclusion not only strengthens the team but also leads to better outcomes, as diverse perspectives are essential for solving complex problems in today's globalized world.

As we navigate the future of work, partnering offers a powerful solution for creating adaptable, inclusive, and innovative teams. Whether working with remote teams, global collaborators, or diverse workforces, partnering principles—collaboration, trust, and shared accountability—are essential for success. In the next chapter, we'll explore the spiritual and energetic dimensions of partnering, showing how these principles can be applied not only to work but to our personal growth and relationships as well. Let's continue this journey of discovering how partnering can transform not only how we work but how we live and connect with others in an increasingly complex world.

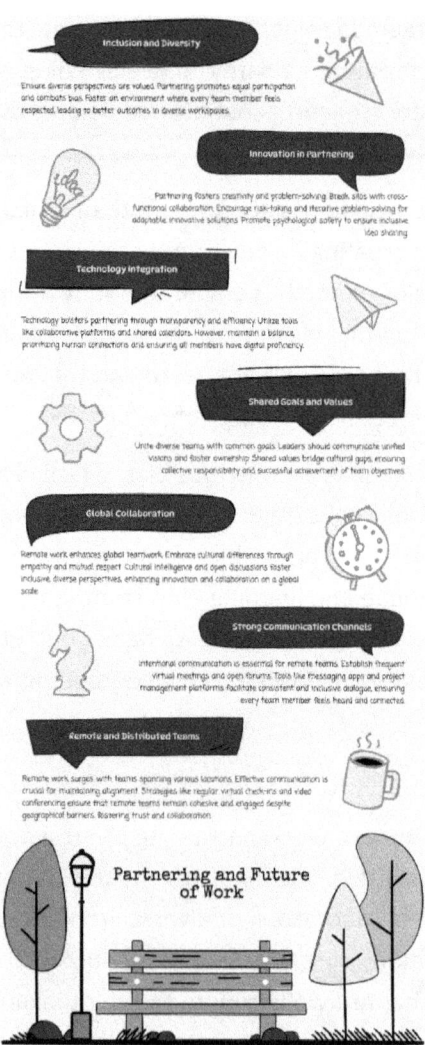

Chapter 9: The Spiritual Aspect – A Holistic View

Throughout this book, we've explored how partnering transforms teams, projects, and leadership. We've seen how collaboration, trust, and shared accountability lead to better outcomes, more cohesive teams, and greater innovation. But partnering is not just a practical tool for improving work environments—it also holds profound spiritual and energetic dimensions. In this chapter, we will explore the deeper, holistic side of partnering, where the principles of unity, empathy, and mutual respect transcend the workplace and permeate our personal lives, relationships, and spiritual growth.

The spiritual aspect of partnering is about recognizing our interconnectedness—not only within teams and organizations but as human beings sharing the same world. It's about cultivating harmony in all areas of life and seeing every interaction as an opportunity for growth and connection. Partnering, in this sense, becomes more than just a strategy for managing work—it becomes a philosophy for living in alignment with our highest selves and the world around us.

9.1 The Energy of Collaboration and Connection

At the core of partnering lies the energy of connection. When we work together in harmony with others, we are tapping into a powerful energetic flow that enhances creativity, productivity, and personal fulfillment. This energy is not just about accomplishing tasks or meeting deadlines—it's about co-creating something greater than the sum of its parts. When teams come together with mutual respect and a shared vision, they generate a positive, uplifting energy that drives success on both practical and spiritual levels.

In many spiritual traditions, this concept of energy flow is understood as **chi** or **prana**—the life force that flows through all living things. When we partner with others in a spirit of collaboration and unity, we align our own energy with this greater flow, creating a sense of ease, balance, and harmony.

Conversely, when we approach teamwork from a place of competition, mistrust, or ego, we block this natural flow and create resistance.

The energy of partnering is also deeply connected to the principle of **giving and receiving**. In a true partnership, there is a balance between offering our talents, skills, and support to others while being open to receiving help, feedback, and guidance in return. This exchange of energy creates a dynamic flow that strengthens relationships and fosters mutual growth. It's important to remember that partnering is not just about what we can give—it's also about being willing to receive, to listen, and to learn from others.

9.2 Cultivating Empathy and Compassion in Partnering

Empathy and compassion are essential components of the spiritual aspect of partnering. When we approach partnerships with empathy, we are able to truly see and understand the experiences, emotions, and needs of others. This deep level of understanding allows us to connect with others on a more meaningful level, fostering trust and collaboration.

Compassion, meanwhile, is the act of recognizing the struggles or challenges of others and responding with kindness and support. In a partnering environment, compassionate leadership involves creating a safe space for team members to express their concerns and emotions without fear of judgment. It also means offering help when needed, providing encouragement, and showing appreciation for the contributions of others.

Empathy and compassion go beyond the workplace. When we embody these qualities in our personal lives, we create deeper, more meaningful connections with family, friends, and our communities. By practicing empathy and compassion in all areas of life, we not only strengthen our relationships but also grow as individuals, becoming more attuned to the needs and experiences of those around us.

In many ways, empathy and compassion are spiritual practices that remind us of our shared humanity. By acknowledging the emotions and experiences of others, we recognize that we are all interconnected and that our actions have a ripple effect on the people and the world around us.

9.3 Partnering with Yourself – A Journey of Inner Growth

Just as partnering with others is essential for collaboration, partnering with yourself is vital for personal growth. The concept of **self-partnering** involves developing a deeper relationship with your own thoughts, emotions, and desires. It's about taking responsibility for your own growth, listening to your inner voice, and aligning your actions with your highest self.

In the same way that you foster trust and communication in partnerships with others, you must also cultivate these qualities within yourself. This means practicing self-awareness, acknowledging your strengths and areas for improvement, and being honest with yourself about your goals and values. It also involves treating yourself with the same empathy and compassion that you extend to others.

Self-partnering is an ongoing practice of checking in with yourself, reflecting on your progress, and making adjustments when necessary. It's about recognizing when you are out of alignment—whether through stress, overwhelm, or disconnection—and taking steps to bring yourself back into harmony. Just as successful teams thrive on regular communication, your relationship with yourself flourishes when you create space for self-reflection and self-care.

At a deeper spiritual level, self-partnering is about recognizing your inherent worth and potential. When you partner with yourself, you tap into your inner wisdom and power, allowing you to move through life with greater clarity, purpose, and confidence.

9.4 The Power of Intention in Partnering

One of the most powerful spiritual principles in partnering is the **power of intention**. In both personal and professional partnerships, setting clear intentions creates a focused, purposeful energy that guides your actions and decisions. When you are intentional in your partnerships, you align your thoughts, words, and actions with your desired outcome, creating a sense of direction and clarity.

In a team setting, intentions can be set collectively, aligning everyone around a common purpose or goal. When all team members are clear on the intention behind their work, they are more likely to stay focused, motivated, and aligned with one another. This collective intention creates a shared energy that drives the project forward with greater efficiency and harmony.

At an individual level, setting intentions can transform the way you approach your work and relationships. By setting intentions for how you want to show up in the world—whether it's with kindness, creativity, or openness—you bring greater awareness and purpose to your actions. Intentions are not about controlling outcomes; rather, they are about aligning yourself with the energy you wish to create and allowing that energy to guide you.

In many spiritual practices, the power of intention is closely linked to **manifestation**—the idea that by focusing your energy and attention on a desired outcome, you can bring it into reality. While this may sound mystical, it's a concept that is grounded in psychology and neuroscience. When you set clear intentions, you activate the part of your brain responsible for filtering information and making decisions, making it more likely that you will take actions aligned with your goals.

9.5 Partnering with the World – A Call for Global Unity

The spiritual dimension of partnering extends beyond individuals and teams—it's about partnering with the world itself. As global citizens, we are all interconnected, and our actions have a direct impact on the planet and future generations. By adopting a partnering mindset in our interactions with the environment, society, and the global community, we can contribute to a more harmonious and sustainable world.

Partnering with the world means recognizing our responsibility to care for the Earth and its resources. It involves making conscious choices that align with the well-being of the planet, whether through sustainable practices, ethical decision-making, or supporting social and environmental causes. It's about seeing ourselves as stewards of the Earth, committed to leaving it better than we found it.

This global perspective is also about fostering **unity and cooperation** among nations, cultures, and communities. In a world that is often divided by conflict, competition, and inequality, partnering offers a path toward greater understanding and collaboration. By embracing the principles of empathy, mutual respect, and shared accountability on a global scale, we can work together to address the challenges facing humanity and create a future of peace, prosperity, and sustainability.

As we embrace the spiritual aspects of partnering, we open ourselves to deeper connections, greater fulfillment, and a sense of purpose that transcends the workplace. In the final chapter, we will explore how the principles of partnering can create a lasting legacy, both personally and professionally. Together, we will discover how partnering not only leads to success in projects and teams but also enriches our lives and strengthens our relationships with ourselves, others, and the world around us. Let's continue this journey of holistic growth, where the power of partnering becomes a guiding force in every area of life.

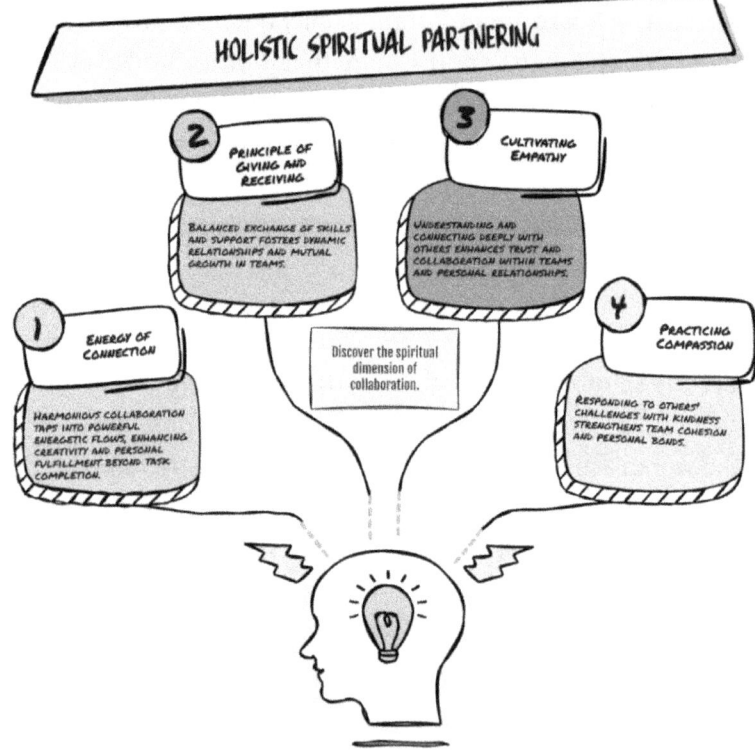

Chapter 10: Creating a Culture
Accountability and Mutual Support

As we reach the final chapter of this journey into the principles of partnering, it's time to explore one of the most crucial aspects of sustainable success: building a culture of accountability and mutual support. In any team, organization, or community, the ability to hold ourselves and each other accountable is vital for ensuring progress, alignment, and integrity. Equally important is the need for a foundation of support, where individuals feel empowered, valued, and trusted to contribute their best.

In this chapter, we will discuss how partnering fosters a culture where accountability and support go hand in hand, creating an environment that nurtures both personal growth and collective success. By blending clear expectations with empathy and mutual trust, partnering becomes the foundation for thriving teams, responsible leadership, and lasting impact. We'll explore practical strategies for creating and sustaining this culture in work environments, as well as its application in personal and community settings.

10.1 The Meaning of Accountability in Partnering

Accountability in a partnering culture is not about micromanaging or placing blame. Instead, it's about shared responsibility and ownership—ensuring that everyone understands their role in contributing to the collective goal and feels empowered to fulfill their commitments. Accountability in partnering is built on trust, clarity, and communication, where expectations are transparent, and team members hold themselves and each other accountable in a spirit of collaboration, not control.

In traditional leadership models, accountability often comes from the top down, where managers enforce deadlines and tasks. But in a partnering environment, accountability is **distributed**. Every member of the team understands that their individual actions impact the whole group, and there's a shared commitment to maintaining high standards of performance and integrity. Leaders in this setting are facilitators, guiding teams toward their goals while supporting their autonomy and growth.

For accountability to work effectively, clear expectations must be set from the start. This means defining roles, responsibilities, and outcomes at the beginning of a project or partnership. It also means creating an open dialogue where team members can communicate their progress, share challenges, and ask for support when needed. When accountability is mutual, it becomes a positive force for progress rather than a source of stress or tension.

10.2 The Role of Trust in Accountability

Trust is the cornerstone of any culture of accountability. Without trust, accountability can quickly turn into blame-shifting or micromanagement, which erodes team morale and reduces overall effectiveness. But when trust is present, team members feel safe to take ownership of their tasks and responsibilities, knowing that they are supported and respected by their peers and leaders.

Building trust requires consistent actions and communication over time. Leaders play a critical role in modeling trust by being transparent about their own goals and challenges, admitting when they make mistakes, and encouraging open communication. By creating a safe space where team members can express concerns or seek help without fear of judgment, leaders help establish a foundation of trust that reinforces accountability.

Mutual trust also allows teams to navigate difficult situations more effectively. When problems arise—whether they are related to project delays, conflicting priorities, or personal challenges—trust enables teams to address these issues head-on, with empathy and a commitment to finding solutions together. In this way, trust transforms accountability into a shared commitment to success, rather than an individual burden.

10.3 Strategies for Building Accountability

Creating a culture of accountability within a team requires intentional effort. Here are some practical strategies for fostering accountability in a partnering environment:

1. **Set Clear Expectations**: From the beginning of any project, ensure that everyone understands their roles, responsibilities, and deadlines. This clarity eliminates confusion and provides a roadmap for success. Make sure to regularly revisit these expectations and adjust them if necessary.

2. **Regular Check-Ins**: Consistent communication is key to maintaining accountability. Schedule regular check-ins with the team to discuss progress, challenges, and any adjustments that need to be made. These meetings should be open and collaborative, not punitive.

3. **Encourage Ownership**: Empower team members to take ownership of their tasks by giving them the autonomy to make decisions and solve problems. When people feel a sense of ownership, they are more likely to hold themselves accountable for their performance.

4. **Provide Constructive Feedback**: Feedback is essential for growth, and in a partnering culture, it should be both regular and constructive. Offer feedback in a way that supports development and improvement, while also encouraging self-reflection and responsibility.

5. **Celebrate Wins and Learn from Setbacks**: Recognize and celebrate team successes, both big and small. Equally important is to treat setbacks as learning opportunities. Instead of focusing on blame, work together to identify what went wrong and how to improve in the future.

10.4 Mutual Support: The Heart of Partnering

While accountability is essential for ensuring progress and results, mutual support is what sustains and enriches a partnering culture. Mutual support means that team members are not only responsible for their own tasks but also for helping each other succeed. This creates a sense of interconnectedness, where the success of one person contributes to the success of the whole.

In a partnering environment, mutual support shows up in many ways: offering help to a colleague who is struggling, sharing resources or knowledge, and providing emotional support during challenging times. This support doesn't just come from leadership—it flows between team members, creating a strong, resilient network where everyone is invested in each other's success.

Supportive teams are more likely to **innovate** and take risks because they know that they have a safety net. When team members feel supported, they are more willing to experiment, share ideas, and take on new challenges without fear of failure. This spirit of collaboration fuels creativity and leads to better problem-solving and decision-making.

Supportive environments also foster **well-being**. In today's fast-paced work culture, burnout and stress are common issues. When teams operate in a culture of mutual support, individuals are less likely to feel isolated or overwhelmed. Instead, they know they can rely on their peers for help, encouragement, and understanding.

10.5 Creating Systems of Support and Accountability

To cultivate both accountability and support, organizations need to implement systems that encourage these behaviors consistently. Here are a few ways to build systems that reinforce a partnering culture:

1. **Peer Accountability Partnerships**: Encourage team members to form accountability partnerships, where they check in with each other on

goals and progress. This can create a sense of shared responsibility and deepen relationships within the team.

2. **Mentorship and Coaching**: Establish formal or informal mentorship programs where experienced team members provide guidance and support to newer or less experienced colleagues. Coaching is another way to offer individualized support, helping people grow within their roles.

3. **Feedback Loops**: Create regular feedback loops where team members can give and receive feedback from peers, leaders, and subordinates. These feedback sessions should focus on both accountability (progress toward goals) and support (areas for growth and development).

4. **Recognition and Reward**: Develop systems for recognizing and rewarding both accountability and support. This could include shout-outs in team meetings, recognition programs, or even bonuses for team-based achievements. Recognizing these behaviors reinforces their importance in the organizational culture.

5. **Flexible and Inclusive Leadership**: Leaders should remain flexible and adaptive to the needs of their teams. By being responsive to individual and collective challenges, leaders can provide the necessary support while also maintaining accountability standards.

10.6 The Long-Term Benefits of a Culture of Accountability and Support

When accountability and support are integrated into the fabric of a team or organization, the long-term benefits are profound. Teams become more **resilient**, able to navigate challenges with confidence and collaboration. Individuals experience **personal growth** as they are held to high standards while being supported in their development. And most importantly, the team as a whole becomes more **aligned and cohesive**, driving long-term success.

Organizations that embrace partnering principles of accountability and mutual support are also better positioned for **sustainable success**. They create environments where people feel valued, respected, and empowered to contribute, leading to higher levels of engagement, retention, and overall job satisfaction.

The impact of these principles extends beyond the workplace. In personal relationships, communities, and even global interactions, the balance of accountability and support fosters trust, growth, and connection. Whether in a small team or a large organization, the culture of partnering has the potential to transform how we interact with one another and how we achieve our shared goals.

As we conclude this book, it's clear that partnering is more than just a strategy for team dynamics or leadership—it's a philosophy for creating harmony, trust, and success in all areas of life. By embracing the principles of collaboration, shared accountability, mutual support, and empathy, we not only improve our professional outcomes but also enhance our personal growth and relationships.

Let this be a call to action: Partner with yourself, partner with others, and partner with the world around you. In doing so, you'll not only achieve more but also live in alignment with the deeper purpose of connection, cooperation, and mutual empowerment. Together, we can create a future where partnering is the foundation for thriving teams, strong leaders, and a more harmonious world.

BUILDING A CULTURE OF ACCOUNTABILITY

Partnering nurtures accountability and support.

DEFINE CLEAR EXPECTATIONS

Establish roles and responsibilities from the project's start to eliminate confusion and provide clear direction. Regularly revisit and adjust these expectations to keep everyone aligned and maintain a focus on the collective goal.

REGULAR CHECK-INS

Frequent check-ins ensure ongoing accountability by providing a platform for discussing progress, challenges, and adjustments. These meetings should be collaborative and open, fostering a team spirit rather than focusing on punitive measures.

ENCOURAGE OWNERSHIP

Giving team members the autonomy to make decisions and solve problems themselves fosters a sense of ownership. This personal investment enhances their responsibility towards their work and the overall performance of the team.

PROVIDE CONSTRUCTIVE FEEDBACK

Regular constructive feedback is crucial for personal and team development. Feedback should support improvement and encourage self-reflection, helping individuals and teams to understand their areas for growth and maintain accountability.

CELEBRATE WINS AND LEARN FROM SETBACKS

Recognizing both small and large successes motivates the team, while treating setbacks as learning opportunities fosters a constructive rather than a blame-oriented culture. This approach encourages continuous improvement and resilience.

PEER ACCOUNTABILITY PARTNERSHIPS

Encouraging team members to form accountability partnerships fosters a shared sense of responsibility. Regular check-ins between peers deepen relationships and ensure continuous progress and support toward shared goals.

MENTORSHIP AND COACHING

Implementing mentorship or coaching programs provides personalized support for personal and professional growth. Experienced team members can offer valuable insights and guidance, strengthening accountability and support within the team.

FLEXIBLE AND INCLUSIVE LEADERSHIP

Leaders must remain adaptive and responsive to individual and collective needs, providing necessary support while maintaining accountability. Flexibility in leadership promotes a supportive environment where team members feel valued and empowered.

Chapter 11: Measuring Success

As we've explored throughout this book, the principles of partnering are designed to foster collaboration, trust, and mutual accountability, all while driving both personal and organizational growth. But how do we measure the success of partnering efforts? How can we assess whether our teams are truly aligned, our projects are progressing, and our relationships are deepening in a meaningful way?

In this chapter, we'll focus on the tangible and intangible ways to measure the success of partnering. We'll introduce tools and strategies to track progress, assess performance, and evaluate both individual and team development. By understanding how to measure success in partnering, we can ensure that the principles we've put into practice are creating long-term positive outcomes, not just in our projects, but also in the growth of individuals and teams. Partnering success isn't just about completing a task— it's about creating a foundation for continuous improvement, resilience, and innovation.

11.1 Defining Success in Partnering

Before diving into specific tools and metrics, it's important to define what success in partnering looks like. Traditional success metrics often focus on project completion, staying on budget, or meeting deadlines. While these outcomes are important, partnering success goes beyond just hitting targets—it's about how those outcomes are achieved and the strength of the relationships formed along the way.

In partnering, success is defined by factors such as:

- **Trust**: Have team members built mutual trust? Do they communicate openly and feel comfortable sharing ideas, concerns, and feedback?

- **Collaboration**: Are individuals and teams working together effectively, or are there still silos or competition? Is there a sense of shared ownership of both successes and challenges?
- **Growth**: Are individuals and teams growing as a result of the partnership? Are they learning new skills, developing leadership abilities, and improving their capacity to work together?
- **Innovation**: Is the partnership fostering creativity and innovation? Are teams able to solve problems in new ways, or have they developed solutions that wouldn't have been possible without collaborative efforts?
- **Sustainability**: Does the partnership create systems and relationships that are sustainable over time? Will the benefits of the partnership last beyond the immediate project, or are they short-lived?

Measuring success in partnering means taking into account not just the end results but also the process and the long-term impact of the collaboration. With these elements in mind, we can then identify the tools and strategies to track success effectively.

11.2 Key Performance Indicators (KPIs) for Partnering Success

To ensure partnering efforts are effective, it's helpful to establish Key Performance Indicators (KPIs) that reflect both the qualitative and quantitative aspects of success. These KPIs provide a clear and consistent way to measure progress and identify areas for improvement. Here are some examples of KPIs that can be used to assess partnering success:

1. **Communication Effectiveness**: Measure the frequency, transparency, and openness of communication among team members. This can be assessed through surveys, feedback loops, or even by tracking the number of productive meetings and shared updates.
2. **Trust Levels**: Assess the level of trust within the team by using anonymous surveys or team-building assessments that ask team

members to evaluate how much they trust their peers and leaders. High trust levels indicate a successful partnering culture.

3. **Collaboration and Engagement**: Track the level of collaboration by monitoring how often team members work together across departments or functions. You can measure this by looking at shared projects, interdepartmental meetings, or collaborative brainstorming sessions.

4. **Innovation Metrics**: Innovation can be tracked by evaluating the number of new ideas generated, the successful implementation of those ideas, and the impact of innovative solutions on project outcomes. Consider using innovation logs or tracking creative problem-solving sessions.

5. **Individual and Team Growth**: Measure personal and team growth through performance reviews, self-assessments, and peer feedback. Growth can be evaluated based on new skills acquired, leadership development, and overall improvement in teamwork dynamics.

6. **Project Outcomes**: While the qualitative aspects of partnering are critical, it's also important to measure traditional project outcomes like timelines, budgets, and deliverables. Ensure that these are tracked alongside the softer metrics to get a holistic view of success.

11.3 Tools for Measuring Success

Now that we've outlined what to measure, let's explore the tools that can help assess partnering success. These tools should not only provide insight into outcomes but also promote reflection, growth, and continuous improvement.

1. **Surveys and Feedback Forms**: Regular anonymous surveys allow team members to share their thoughts on communication, trust, and collaboration within the team. These surveys should ask specific questions about the team's effectiveness, how supported individuals

feel, and any areas for improvement. Tools like Google Forms, Typeform, or SurveyMonkey can be easily implemented to gather this data.

2. **Project Management Tools**: Platforms like Asana, Trello, and Monday.com allow teams to track the progress of tasks and projects. These tools can provide insight into how well teams are collaborating, meeting deadlines, and communicating. By reviewing task completion rates and monitoring project milestones, leaders can assess both the efficiency and cohesion of the team.

3. **Peer Review Systems**: Implementing a peer review system allows team members to evaluate each other's contributions and offer constructive feedback. This fosters a culture of mutual accountability and support. Platforms like 15Five or Lattice can facilitate peer reviews and self-assessments that align with partnering principles.

4. **Innovation Logs**: Encourage teams to keep innovation logs where they track new ideas, solutions, and brainstorming sessions. These logs serve as a way to document creative thinking and innovation in real-time. At the end of a project or milestone, review the logs to evaluate how partnering fostered innovative outcomes.

5. **Growth and Development Tracking**: Regular performance reviews, one-on-one meetings, and professional development plans are important tools for measuring individual and team growth. Leaders can track progress in leadership skills, collaboration, and communication, using platforms like BambooHR or Workday to monitor personal development over time.

6. **Qualitative Reflection Sessions**: Beyond formal reviews and surveys, periodic reflection sessions allow teams to openly discuss their partnering experience. In these sessions, teams can reflect on what's working, what's not, and how they can improve going forward.

Facilitated discussions, guided by specific reflection prompts, offer rich qualitative insights into the team's dynamics and progress.

11.4 Evaluating Long-Term Impact

While immediate project outcomes are important, partnering success should also be measured by its **long-term impact**. This involves assessing how well the relationships, systems, and practices developed through partnering continue to benefit the team and organization over time.

One way to evaluate long-term impact is to look at **sustainability metrics**. Are the partnerships formed during a specific project continuing to thrive in future projects? Are the lessons learned being applied to new challenges? Has the team's ability to collaborate improved beyond the scope of the original project?

Another long-term indicator is the **retention and engagement** of team members. Teams that embrace partnering often have higher levels of job satisfaction, engagement, and retention. Tracking these metrics over time provides valuable insight into the lasting benefits of a partnering culture.

Leaders can also conduct **post-project reviews** several months or even a year after a project is completed. These reviews provide an opportunity to reflect on the long-term outcomes of partnering efforts, identify areas for further growth, and celebrate the ongoing success of the team.

11.5 Continuous Improvement and Iteration

One of the core principles of partnering is the idea of **continuous improvement**. No partnership is ever static—there is always room for growth, reflection, and refinement. Measuring success in partnering isn't just about determining whether a project was successful; it's about asking, "How can we do even better next time?"

Partnering encourages teams to take a **growth mindset** approach, viewing challenges and setbacks as opportunities to learn and improve. After each project or milestone, teams should engage in a process of reflection and iteration. What worked well? What could be improved? What new tools, strategies, or practices could enhance the next phase of the project?

This culture of continuous improvement creates an environment where learning is valued, and individuals are encouraged to experiment, innovate, and grow together. By using the metrics and tools outlined in this chapter, teams can assess their progress and make meaningful adjustments that lead to long-term success.

Measuring success in partnering goes far beyond traditional metrics like project completion and budget adherence. It's about evaluating the **quality of relationships**, the **depth of collaboration**, and the **growth** of both individuals and teams. By using a combination of qualitative and quantitative tools, we can ensure that partnering efforts not only achieve short-term goals but also create lasting impact and continuous improvement.

As we conclude this chapter, remember that partnering is not a one-time solution—it's a philosophy for sustained success. Whether in personal relationships, professional teams, or broader communities, the principles of partnering—trust, accountability, empathy, and collaboration—can transform the way we work and live. With the right tools in place, you can measure and celebrate the success of your partnerships, while continually striving for even greater growth and harmony in the future.

MEASURING SUCCESS IN PARTNERING

DEFINE SUCCESS IN PARTNERING
Success encompasses outcomes and relationship quality, including trust, collaboration, growth, innovation, and sustainability. It's not just finishing a task but creating an enduring foundation for continuous improvement, resilience, and innovation. Establishing a clear definition aids in identifying accurate metrics.

TRUST LEVELS
Assess trust through anonymous surveys or team-building assessments, gauging the mutual trust among peers and leaders. High trust levels are indicative of a successful partnership and sustainable collaboration, where individuals feel secure and valued in contributing ideas.

COMMUNICATION EFFECTIVENESS
Measure using surveys, feedback loops, and tracking productive meetings. Effective communication promotes transparency, alignment, and a sense of shared ownership, significantly enhancing collaboration and ensuring that challenges are addressed promptly and efficiently.

COLLABORATION AND ENGAGEMENT
Track teamwork across departments and functions. High levels of collaboration signify a dismantling of silos, promoting shared ownership and diverse problem-solving approaches that enrich team dynamics and project outcomes.

INNOVATION METRICS
Track new ideas, their implementation, and resultant impact using innovation logs. These metrics highlight how effectively the partnership fosters creative solutions, reflecting both the process and results of collaborative efforts.

PROJECT MANAGEMENT TOOLS
Use platforms like Asana or Trello for task and progress tracking. These tools offer insights into team efficiency, collaboration quality, and project milestone achievements, facilitating continuous monitoring and adjustment.

GROWTH AND DEVELOPMENT TRACKING
Regular performance reviews and professional development plans should track skill acquisition and leadership growth. Monitoring these metrics ensures that both individuals and teams are continually developing, enhancing their capacity to collaborate effectively.

CONTINUOUS IMPROVEMENT
Engage in reflection and iteration post-project. Assess what worked or failed and adopt new strategies for future projects. This growth mindset fosters a culture where learning and innovation thrive, driving sustained success in partnering.

Chapter 12: The Legacy of Partnering
A Blueprint for Future Projects

As we come to the final chapter of this book, it's important to reflect on the lasting legacy that partnering can create—not only within teams and organizations but also in the broader context of leadership, community, and personal growth. Partnering is more than just a set of strategies; it's a philosophy, a way of being that transcends projects and reaches into the core of how we interact with others and the world.

This chapter will focus on how partnering principles leave a lasting impact on teams, individuals, and organizations long after a project is completed. We'll explore how partnering builds stronger relationships, creates a blueprint for future success, and sets the stage for continuous improvement and innovation. By embracing partnering as a lifelong practice, leaders can create a legacy of collaboration, trust, and shared accountability that extends far beyond the immediate goals of any one project.

12.1 Building a Legacy of Strong Relationships

One of the most significant outcomes of partnering is the strength of the relationships it fosters. Partnering is about more than just completing a task—it's about building trust, mutual respect, and deep connections between individuals. These relationships are the foundation of long-term success, both for the team and for the organization as a whole.

When teams work in a partnering environment, they develop a sense of shared purpose that goes beyond the specific goals of a project. They learn to trust each other, communicate openly, and support one another's growth. These relationships don't just dissolve once the project is over; they endure, creating a strong network of collaboration that can be leveraged in future projects.

The legacy of these relationships extends beyond the workplace as well. Partnering principles, such as empathy, accountability, and mutual respect, can transform the way individuals interact with their families, communities, and social networks. By fostering deeper, more meaningful relationships in all areas of life, partnering creates a ripple effect that enhances personal and professional well-being.

Leaders who embrace partnering leave behind a legacy of **trust**. Teams that have experienced true partnering are more likely to continue working in a collaborative, supportive manner, even when faced with new challenges. The bonds created through partnering ensure that teams are resilient, adaptable, and prepared to navigate future projects with confidence and success.

12.2 Creating a Blueprint for Future Success

One of the most powerful aspects of partnering is its ability to create a **blueprint for future projects**. When teams successfully implement partnering principles, they establish systems, processes, and behaviors that can be replicated and refined in future initiatives. This blueprint becomes a guide for how teams can continue to work together effectively, regardless of the specifics of the project.

The lessons learned from partnering efforts provide valuable insights into what works—and what doesn't—in terms of collaboration, communication, and accountability. These insights can be documented and shared with other teams or departments, creating a culture of continuous learning and improvement. By building on the successes of previous projects, organizations can develop a **framework** for partnering that evolves over time, adapting to new challenges and opportunities.

This blueprint is particularly valuable for leaders who are tasked with managing complex, cross-functional projects. By applying the principles of partnering, leaders can create a **repeatable process** that ensures alignment, trust, and collaboration across teams. Whether it's a construction project, a product launch, or a long-term strategic initiative, partnering provides a proven approach for achieving success while fostering a positive, collaborative work environment.

12.3 The Long-Term Benefits of Partnering

The benefits of partnering extend far beyond the immediate outcomes of a project. While successful partnering leads to better communication, trust, and accountability in the short term, its long-term impact is even more profound. When organizations fully embrace partnering, they create a culture where collaboration is the norm, not the exception.

Teams that operate in a partnering culture are more **engaged, motivated,** and **innovative**. They feel a sense of ownership over their work and are more likely to take initiative, propose creative solutions, and invest in the success of the organization. This increased engagement leads to higher job satisfaction and retention, as individuals feel more connected to their teams and to the organization's mission.

In the long term, partnering also promotes **organizational resilience**. Teams that have learned to work together through partnering are better equipped to handle change, uncertainty, and challenges. They have developed the communication skills, trust, and problem-solving abilities necessary to navigate difficult situations with grace and confidence.

Organizations that prioritize partnering are also more likely to attract and retain **top talent**. In today's competitive job market, individuals are looking for workplaces that prioritize collaboration, respect, and personal growth. By fostering a partnering culture, organizations create an environment where people want to work—a place where they feel valued, supported, and empowered to contribute to meaningful goals.

12.4 Partnering as a Lifelong Practice

While partnering is often discussed in the context of projects and teams, it's also a **lifelong practice** that extends beyond the workplace. The principles of partnering—collaboration, empathy, trust, and shared accountability—are applicable in all areas of life, from personal relationships to community involvement.

By adopting a partnering mindset in our everyday interactions, we can create more harmonious, fulfilling relationships. Whether it's working through conflicts with a spouse, collaborating with neighbors on a community project, or supporting a friend in need, partnering teaches us how to communicate openly, listen with empathy, and work together toward common goals.

At its core, partnering is about **connection**—connection with others, with ourselves, and with the world around us. It's a philosophy that encourages us to see beyond our individual desires and consider the greater good, to build relationships based on trust and mutual respect, and to take responsibility for our actions and their impact on others.

For leaders, embracing partnering as a lifelong practice means applying these principles not just in their professional roles but in all areas of life. It's about leading with empathy, supporting the growth of others, and fostering environments where collaboration and innovation thrive.

12.5 Passing the Torch: Mentorship and Leadership Development

One of the most important aspects of creating a lasting legacy through partnering is the act of **passing the torch**. Leaders who have embraced partnering have a responsibility to mentor and develop the next generation of leaders. By sharing their knowledge, experience, and insights, they ensure that the principles of partnering continue to shape the future of teams and organizations.

Mentorship is a powerful way to instill the values of partnering in emerging leaders. Through one-on-one coaching, regular feedback, and open dialogue, leaders can help others understand the importance of trust, accountability, and collaboration. By modeling partnering behaviors and offering guidance on how to implement these principles, mentors can empower the next generation to lead with empathy and effectiveness.

In addition to mentorship, organizations should prioritize **leadership development programs** that emphasize partnering principles. These programs can provide training on communication, conflict resolution, emotional intelligence, and collaborative decision-making, equipping future leaders with the tools they need to succeed in a partnering environment.

By investing in leadership development, organizations ensure that partnering becomes a core part of their culture for years to come. Leaders who have learned to work in a partnering model are more likely to foster collaboration, build strong relationships, and drive innovation in their teams, creating a positive cycle of growth and success.

As we close this book, it's clear that partnering is more than just a method for completing projects—it's a transformative philosophy that has the power to shape the way we lead, work, and live. By embracing the principles of partnering, we create a legacy of trust, collaboration, and mutual support that extends far beyond the immediate goals of any one project.

This legacy is not just about what we achieve in the short term—it's about how we build the foundation for long-term success, resilience, and growth. Whether in teams, organizations, or personal relationships, partnering offers a blueprint for creating a more connected, harmonious world.

Let this be your call to action: embrace partnering as a lifelong practice, share it with others, and continue to build a legacy of collaboration, trust, and shared accountability. By doing so, you'll not only achieve your own goals but also contribute to a brighter, more connected future for everyone around you.

The Legacy of Partnering

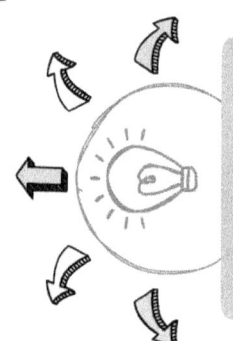

01 Building Strong Relationships
Partnering fosters trust and mutual respect, creating enduring connections that extend beyond individual projects. This builds strong foundations for long-term success, both within the team and the broader organization, encouraging open communication, support, and a network of collaboration for future endeavors.

02 Blueprint for Success
Successful partnering creates replicable systems and processes for future projects. By documenting and sharing insights, organizations promote continuous learning and improvement, ensuring a proven, adaptable approach to collaboration and achieving success across diverse and complex initiatives.

03 Long-Term Benefits
Partnering promotes engagement, innovation, and resilience. Teams in a partnering culture take initiative, propose creative solutions, and feel connected to their organization's mission, leading to higher job satisfaction, retention, and the ability to navigate challenges effectively.

04 Lifelong Practice
Partnering principles are applicable in all areas of life. By adopting collaboration, empathy, and trust, individuals create meaningful relationships, fostering a philosophy that emphasizes the greater good, mutual respect, and shared responsibility beyond the workplace.

05 Mentorship and Leadership Development
Leaders should mentor and develop new leaders by sharing partnering principles. Effective mentorship empowers emerging leaders with the values of trust, accountability, and collaboration, ensuring these principles shape the future of teams and organizations.

06 Empathy and Communication
Partnering emphasizes empathy and open communication. This fosters a deeper understanding among team members, enabling effective conflict resolution and collaborative decision-making, which strengthens team dynamics and improves overall project outcomes.

07 Shared Accountability
In a partnering environment, all team members are accountable. Shared accountability ensures that everyone takes responsibility for their roles and contributions, promoting a sense of ownership that drives team success and reliability.

08 Attracting Top Talent
Organizations with a partnering culture are more appealing. By prioritizing collaboration, respect, and personal growth, these organizations attract and retain top talent, creating an environment where employees feel valued and motivated to contribute to meaningful goals.

Chapter 13: A Path to Collective Transformation

As we reach the conclusion of this book, it's time to reflect on the deeper meaning of partnering. Throughout the chapters, we've explored how partnering can improve teams, projects, and leadership. But beyond the tangible results, partnering offers something more profound: a path to collective transformation. This final chapter is a call to action—to embrace partnering as a way of living and a vehicle for creating lasting change in the world.

Partnering isn't just a strategy for the workplace; it's a mindset that can guide every interaction we have, both personally and professionally. It invites us to connect more deeply with others, to align with a shared purpose, and to work together toward the greater good. By adopting the principles of trust, empathy, accountability, and collaboration, we open ourselves to greater fulfillment, growth, and harmony in all areas of life.

This chapter is an invitation to take what you've learned and apply it in every context—from your personal relationships to your professional endeavors, from local communities to global initiatives. Partnering is not a one-time act; it is a lifelong practice that has the power to transform not only how we work but how we live and connect with others. Now is the time to make partnering a guiding force in your life, leading to both personal growth and collective success.

13.1 Partnering with Yourself for Personal Transformation

Before you can truly partner with others, you must first partner with yourself. Self-partnering means cultivating self-awareness, embracing your strengths and weaknesses, and committing to your personal growth. It's about holding yourself accountable for your actions and aligning your life with your core values.

Start by taking time to reflect on your goals, motivations, and personal aspirations. What do you want to achieve, and how can you best serve yourself and others in the process? Self-partnering involves a balance between self-compassion and self-discipline. Recognize your worth, while also challenging yourself to grow.

Here are some ways to begin self-partnering:

- **Self-Reflection**: Regularly assess where you are in life and where you want to go. Journaling, meditation, or simply taking quiet time to reflect can help you gain clarity and set intentions.
- **Accountability**: Hold yourself accountable to the goals you've set. Acknowledge when you fall short, but instead of self-criticism, use those moments as opportunities to learn and improve.
- **Self-Care**: Treat yourself with the same empathy and compassion you offer others. Prioritize your mental, emotional, and physical well-being to maintain the energy needed to contribute fully in your partnerships.

By partnering with yourself, you build a solid foundation that allows you to enter relationships with others from a place of wholeness, authenticity, and strength.

13.2 Applying Partnering Principles to Your Professional Life

In the workplace, partnering principles can transform teams, leadership styles, and organizational cultures. Whether you are a team leader or a contributor, adopting a partnering mindset fosters an environment of collaboration, innovation, and mutual respect.

For leaders, this means shifting from a traditional command-and-control model to a facilitative role. Empower your team members by providing them with the support, trust, and autonomy to do their best work. Create spaces for open communication and problem-solving. Lead with empathy and foster a sense of shared responsibility for outcomes.

For team members, this means taking ownership of your role within the collective effort. Practice transparency, communicate openly with your colleagues, and actively contribute to the team's success. Hold yourself accountable for your actions, and offer help and support to your peers.

Organizations that embrace partnering create workplaces where individuals feel valued, respected, and engaged. They foster environments where collaboration is celebrated, and where teams work together to achieve goals that benefit both the organization and the individuals within it.

13.3 Partnering in Personal Relationships

Partnering is equally powerful in personal relationships. Whether with family, friends, or romantic partners, the principles of trust, empathy, and accountability are key to building lasting, meaningful connections.

In personal relationships, partnering means:

- **Open Communication**: Be honest and transparent with those closest to you. Share your thoughts and feelings openly, and listen actively to the perspectives of others.
- **Mutual Support**: Recognize that healthy relationships are built on a foundation of mutual support. Be there for others in their times of need, and allow them to support you in return.
- **Shared Accountability**: Take responsibility for your role in conflicts or challenges within the relationship. Work together to find solutions that are beneficial for all parties.

By bringing a partnering mindset into your personal life, you'll strengthen your relationships and create deeper bonds rooted in trust and mutual respect.

13.4 Global Partnering – Becoming a Force for Collective Change

In today's interconnected world, the challenges we face—whether social, environmental, or political—demand collective action and global collaboration. Partnering principles can be a guiding force for addressing these global challenges and becoming a more effective global citizen.

Global partnering involves recognizing the interconnectedness of all people and working together to create solutions that benefit humanity as a whole. Whether through supporting social justice initiatives, promoting environmental sustainability, or advocating for peace, global partnering requires empathy, inclusion, and shared responsibility.

Here are some ways to practice global partnering:

- **Collaboration**: Seek out opportunities to collaborate with individuals, organizations, and communities from diverse backgrounds. This cross-cultural collaboration brings fresh perspectives and solutions to complex problems.
- **Advocacy**: Use your voice and platform to support causes that promote equality, sustainability, and human rights. Stand with others who are working for positive change.
- **Environmental Stewardship**: Recognize your responsibility as a steward of the Earth. Take actions, both big and small, that contribute to the well-being of the planet and future generations.

By practicing global partnering, you can contribute to creating a world where collaboration, empathy, and sustainability are at the core of collective decision-making.

13.5 Creating a Legacy of Partnering – Paying It Forward

As you embrace partnering in your own life, remember the importance of passing these principles on to others. Whether through mentorship, teaching, or simply living by example, you have the power to influence the next generation of leaders, teams, and communities.

Mentorship is a powerful way to share the lessons of partnering. By guiding others, offering support, and sharing your experiences, you help others embrace the values of collaboration, empathy, and trust. Invest in the growth of those around you, and encourage them to adopt a partnering mindset in their own endeavors.

In addition to mentorship, leadership development programs and team training can instill partnering principles within organizations. By teaching the skills of collaboration, communication, and emotional intelligence, you ensure that partnering becomes embedded in the fabric of your workplace or community.

By paying it forward, you leave behind a legacy of trust, empathy, and shared accountability—a legacy that will continue to shape the future of teams, organizations, and communities for years to come.

Final Call to Action

The journey of partnering doesn't end here. It begins with the choice to embrace the principles of collaboration, trust, and mutual accountability as a way of life. As you move forward, take the lessons of this book and apply them to every area of your life—your work, your relationships, and your community.

Partner with yourself. Partner with others. Partner with the world. Through this approach, you can create positive change, build deeper connections, and contribute to a more harmonious, thriving world.

Let partnering be your guide in all that you do. By adopting these principles, you will not only achieve your own goals but also create a ripple effect that inspires others to lead with empathy, collaborate with integrity, and contribute to the greater good.

Together, through partnering, we can transform teams, relationships, and the world at large. The power is in your hands—now it's time to put it into action.

EMBRACE PARTNERING FOR TRANSFORMATION

SELF-REFLECTION
Regularly assess life's direction. Journaling, meditation, or quiet reflection can provide clarity and set intentions.

ACCOUNTABILITY
Hold yourself accountable. Use setbacks as learning opportunities rather than indulging in self-criticism.

SELF-CARE
Prioritize mental, emotional, and physical well-being. Empathy and compassion for yourself fuel sustained partnerships.

LEADERSHIP SHIFTS
Move from command-and-control to a facilitative leadership style. Empower teams through trust and open communication.

OPEN COMMUNICATION
Be honest and transparent with loved ones. Share thoughts and feelings openly to build deeper connections.

About the Author: Zen Benefiel

Zen Benefiel is a multifaceted visionary, author, coach, and speaker with a passion for helping individuals and organizations unlock their highest potential through collaboration, innovation, and holistic growth. With decades of experience in transformational leadership, project management, and personal development, Zen has dedicated his life to creating environments where people and ideas can thrive.

Holding an MA in Organizational Management, a MBA and a Secondary Teaching Certification, Zen has built a diverse career that spans corporate consulting, education, event production, and holistic coaching. He is the founder of **Team Partnering LLC**, where he works with businesses to foster teamwork and cross-functional collaboration through the principles of partnering. Zen has also served as a facilitator for large-scale projects, including major public events, where his leadership helped ensure success by aligning teams, resources, and goals.

In addition to his professional work, Zen is the host of the podcast **One World in a New World**, where he engages thought leaders from around the globe in conversations about consciousness, innovation, and the future of humanity. Through his podcast, Zen explores how personal and collective transformation can lead to a more harmonious world.

A lifelong learner and spiritual seeker, Zen integrates his personal journey into his work, offering a unique perspective that combines practical leadership strategies with deep insights into human connection and self-awareness. As a holistic coach, he has guided countless individuals on their path to self-discovery, helping them align their personal values with their professional goals.

Zen's commitment to partnering extends beyond the workplace. His approach to leadership and team-building is rooted in empathy, trust, and shared accountability—principles that he believes can transform not only businesses but also personal relationships and communities. Whether through his coaching, consulting, or public speaking, Zen empowers others to embrace collaboration as a pathway to greater success and fulfillment.

Zen Benefiel's work is a testament to the power of partnering in all aspects of life. He continues to inspire individuals and organizations to adopt a collaborative mindset, create meaningful connections, and build a brighter, more sustainable future.

For more information on Zen Benefiel, his services, or his podcast, visit his website at **ZenBenefiel.com**.

www.ingramcontent.com/pod-product-compliance
Lightning Source LLC
Chambersburg PA
CBHW070342230526
45471CB00006B/2415